The Art of Reading

Becoming a wiser person

Matthew Porter

Authentic

First published 2026 by Authentic Media Limited,
PO Box 6326, Bletchley, Milton Keynes, MK1 9GG.
authenticmedia.co.uk

EU GPSR Authorised Representative
LOGOS EUROPE, 9 rue Nicolas Poussin, 17000, LA ROCHELLE, France
E-mail: contact@logoseurope.eu

British Library Cataloguing in Publication Data
A catalogue record for this book is available from the British Library.
ISBN: 978-1-78893-371-1
978-1-78893-372-8 (e-book)

Cover design by Henry Milne
Printed and bound by CPI Group (UK) Ltd, Croydon, CR0 4YY

The Art of Reading is like a shortcut to gaining wisdom! What Matthew offers us in just a few pages is potent in both spiritual and practical ways. Each page has encouragement and advice which you can take to heart and apply immediately. He manages to draw a wide range of people in to this subject on which he feels passionately and communicates beautifully. I am already a better reader from reading this brilliant little book.

The Rt Revd Adam Atkinson, Bishop of Bradwell, Diocese of Chelmsford; co-author of Who Do You Say I Am?

In this short but informative book Matthew Porter shows the importance of reading as food for the soul and the mind. As a life-long and avid devourer of books I have been challenged to be a deeper, more intentional reader and now have my pencil at the ready.

The Revd Rachel Watts, Director of Vocations, Diocese of Manchester

I was always taught that 'leaders are readers'. I think that is true for everyone, especially for anyone who wants to be a disciple of Jesus, because we are called to go deep and get beneath the surface of things. Reading exposes us to wisdom, offers perspectives which challenge our limited thinking, and enables us to learn from the experience of others. This book not only inspired me to read more but gave me skills to read more effectively for greater benefit!

Matthew's excellent short book on the what, when, how and why of reading is deeply inspiring. It is packed with practical guidance for developing the art of reading, gleaned from years of personal experience, and also invites readers to be transformed – growing in wisdom and becoming agents of meaningful change.

Matthew Porter writes as a wise friend to encourage us all to read, and to read well. He has a marvellous vision for this, which he communicates in a down-to-earth and practical way, drawing on a wide range of authors and thinkers, as well as his own excitement and experience. This is a short book, but full of things to take on board and put into practice for those who are experienced readers as well as those just starting out or overcoming obstacles in their own reading.

Contents

Preface

This book is written to help followers of Jesus become more prayerful through the practice of reading.

It is called *The Art of Reading* because discipleship – the daily practice of following Jesus – is more an art than a science. It's not a technical process, based on logic or analytical deduction. It's not about rigidly adhering to laws or rules about behaviour or piety. It's more like learning a musical instrument, or discovering how to paint, both of which require patient practice. You have to give yourself to it: particularly your energy and emotions, as well as your time and talents. This is the stretching and adventurous life of discipleship into which followers of Jesus are invited, empowered by the Holy Spirit. It's thoroughly relational – loving God and loving people – and beautifully creative, cultivating habits of the heart which result in a lifestyle that brings lasting transformation to us and to the world. Eugene H. Peterson, author of *The Message* version of the Bible, summarised such a life as learning 'the unforced rhythms of grace' (Matt. 11:28–30 MSG).

This book, in *The Art of* series, is about a particular rhythmic feature of discipleship – *The Art of Reading*. In a few pages the habit is explained and explored, with readers encouraged to practise this art in order to mature and impact the world. I think you will enjoy it. But most of all I hope this habit helps you become a more fruitful and fulfilled missional disciple of Jesus.

The Art of Reading is the fourth in a series of books about discipleship habits.

Matthew Porter
Bishop of Bolton

Introduction

- *'Philip ran up to the chariot and heard the man reading Isaiah the prophet. "Do you understand what you are reading?" Philip asked' (Acts 8:30).*

- *'Books can be dangerous. The best ones should be labelled "This could change your life"' (Helen Exley).*[1]

- *'By lending words to our bewildering experience, books become compasses' (Alberto Manguel).*[2]

- *'nobody gives much attention or energy to teaching how to read' (Eugene Peterson).*[3]

We don't all read alike. It took me twenty-five years to realise this. When I saw someone reading I assumed they read exactly as I did, until I discovered that there were other ways to read a book which I'd never considered. So in this short book I address a number of questions about reading by explaining how and why I read, in the hope it might help others read better, enjoy reading more, and get the most out of books, in order to live an impactful life.

This book in *The Art of* series will especially help followers of Jesus who want to grow through practicing good discipleship habits – and reading is one such discipline. Nevertheless, the book is also written with a wider readership in mind, for the ideas and advice can be applied broadly, and used not just by Christ-followers but by advocates of all religions or none.

Now well into my fifties, I've been on a reading odyssey for much of my life, and I want it to continue until the day I die. One thing I've discovered on the journey is that there's an art to reading which requires continued crafting and developing. As I've grown as a reader, so I love reading more than ever. That's my desire for all who read this short book.

Virtually everyone in the West today reads daily, with most reading more than they realise. Think about it: we read news articles and social media feeds on our phones; signs as we travel; emails and documents as we work; bills so we pay them correctly; newspapers and magazines for information, as well as books for pleasure. Many also read for prayer and reflection, recognising the presence of God and the wonder of the world. But few think about *how* they read, and whether they could read more effectively. Eugene Peterson, the pastor and acclaimed writer/translator of *The Message* paraphrase of the Bible, whose writings have hugely impacted many, including Bono of the band U2, felt the same. He wrote: 'despite the money and time our society expends in teaching us to read, nobody gives much attention or energy to teaching *how* to read', noting that for our ancestors, good reading always 'has wisdom for its goal'.[4] In Chapter 4 of this book I similarly propose, with Peterson, that wisdom should be the aim of our reading.

I'd never considered *how* to read until one day in my mid-twenties I came across an old cassette of a talk by the American minister, Rick Warren, and pushed play.[5] I remember the recording quality was poor, and I think it was entitled, 'How to Read'. I cannot now recall much detail about it, but I know it included all sorts of advice on how to get the most out of reading. It included practical reading tips that I'd never heard anyone talk about before, and it literally changed the way I read. Maybe some of his advice will come out in this book, as Rick Warren's reflections on reading certainly played a big part in re-shaping my thinking and practice at the time.

Since then I've continued to develop the way I read, especially as I read books now much more than I used to. These days I quite often find myself talking with people about how I read, and in the same way that I was helped by Warren, I've been told that sharing my reading experience has helped others. Recently, for example, a friend who is a head teacher told me that our conversation about reading had 'changed her life' and now she reads in a whole new way, and loves it. She's now become an evangelist for this, telling others to read more intentionally and attentively, and urging them to work on how they read. So this book is an attempt to share some of these things that I've discovered so far about *The Art of Reading*. There are no doubt lots of other ways to read, and I'm not suggesting that the way I do it is how everyone should. Rather, I want to share some of my learning, in the hope it might be of some help to others to grow in wisdom.

This is not a book about literacy – about how humans learn to read by developing their phonical awareness as they relate sounds to spelling patterns. Literacy is important, and I'm encouraged to see literacy rates rising across the world, including the UK.[6] Neither is it a book suggesting there are strict rules to reading.[7] Rather, I'm writing to help those who are already readers become better at reading. So if you want to appreciate reading more, read on. If you want to remember more of what you read, read on. If you want your reading to help you become a more well-rounded and mature human being, read on. If finance is tight and you find buying books too expensive, read on. If you want your reading to shape your faith, read on. This is a book for you.

This book is part of a series of six on habits. It was Thomas Aquinas who said that virtues require habits to develop and sustain them. This book is based on the premise that if you want to develop the virtue of wisdom, then learn *The Art of Reading*. As I've talked with people about this series, a number have said that they're particularly looking forward to this one, wanting to get stronger and go deeper in reading. That's good. That's actually what I've found as I've written it. Researching and writing about reading has helped me reflect further on why I read as I do, how I do it, and ways that I might improve. So while I'm putting pen to paper (so to speak) and explaining what I do, I'm still developing as a reader. I recognise that I still have much to learn.

This is not an academic book on the nature of reading. Others have done that, writing excellent books on how books came into being,[8] on why it's good to read,[9] on the craft of reading[10] and on the philosophy of reading.[11] This is instead a simple and, I trust, helpful 'how to' book – explaining what I do when I read, and why it's transformative. At times I will describe very practically some of the things I do when reading. In writing like this, I'm not telling readers that they must do as I do. I'm simply unpacking what I do, as few people describe *how* they read. I hope among the practical tips that there'll be much useful information and many ideas that will make the reader think. But most of all I'm writing to encourage readers to develop their reading skills, because there is much evidence to show that in the UK, like many countries, we are not good at helping children and adults become better readers.[12] As such, the purpose of this book is to equip and empower. Emotionally intelligent writers understand this, with fiction author Flannery O'Connor expressing something of this when saying that her task as a writer was to enable people to experience 'encouragement, consolation, fear, charm, all you demand – and, perhaps, also that glimpse of truth for which you have forgotten to ask'.[13] All good writing should do that. In fact that's one of the main reasons we read – in order to grow. I agree with Victor Hugo, who said, 'To learn to read is to light a fire; every syllable that is spelled out is a spark.'[14] Reading, then, should inflame us to become better human beings, to become more the people God created us to be, so we can make a difference in the world. In short, it's good to improve our reading skills because reading changes us, so we can change others.

This is not a detailed book about reading the Bible. The Bible is regularly referenced, for as a follower of Jesus I consider it to be the most important, helpful and formative book of all. Indeed, in Chapter 4 I offer five models of reading Scripture that I've found impactful over the years, which readers are encouraged to practice. But I go on to suggest those models can be used more broadly, and not just by Christians, as they help us read all texts. That's because the things we learn about following Jesus, especially from the Bible, are not meant to be confined to some narrow Christian segment of our lives; they're meant for the *whole* of life. And to be shared with others. It's what being a Christian – someone committed to whole-life discipleship – is meant to be all about.

If we step back and consider the impact of books, reading, and words, then many, like Jewish rabbi Jonathan Sacks, think 'our very humanity has to do with our ability to use language' which is why Sacks concludes that 'Language is life'.[15] It's through words and reading that our imagination expands, our knowledge increases, and our character develops.[16] Reading expert Damon Young agrees, highlighting a number of character-virtues which good reading can produce in the reader, including curiosity, patience, courage, pride, temperance and justice,[17] and there are many more. Character development is crucial to life and, as Templeton scholar and Professor of Philosophy Christian B. Miller has shown, one of the main sources of virtuous character is found in religious faith, especially Christianity.[18] There's a long tradition, across a breadth of Christian streams, of encouraging good reading to build wise character. This is why reading is so helpful in Christian discipleship, helping people mature in faith and impact culture. So if you're reading this as a follower of Jesus, or a potential follower, may you put into practice many of the things suggested in this book and find yourself being transformed into an even more effective missionary disciple of Jesus Christ.

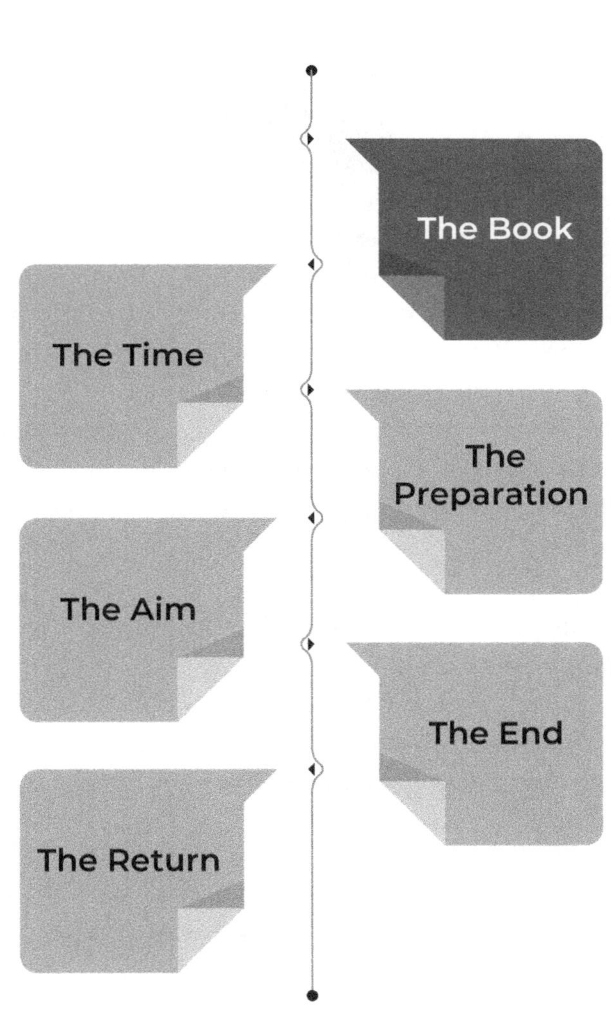

The Book
The Time
The Preparation
The Aim
The End
The Return

Chapter 1

Choose with curiosity

- *'When you come, bring the cloak that I left with Carpus at Troas, also the books' (2 Tim. 4:13, ESV).*

- *'Books help us understand who we are and how we are to behave. They show us what community and friend-ship mean; they show us how to live and die' (Anne Lamott).*[1]

- *'I read a book one day and my whole life was changed' (Orhan Pamuk).*[2]

- *'every choice is a thousand renunciations. To choose one thing is to turn one's back on many others' (Sarah Yardley).*[3]

I was strolling through the streets of Manchester recently, on my way to meet someone. I was slightly early and so in no hurry and found myself gazing into shop windows and doing some people-watching. A pedestrian came towards me and passed by, and I found myself surprisingly animated. It wasn't anything about the person which stood out, it's what they were carrying. They were walking with a book in hand. I was surprised how the scene captured my attention, but it did. It really did. It made me wonder about this person and their priorities. I thought to myself: they're going to read. Or maybe they've been reading, perhaps a few moments ago. They can only carry a few things, and yet they're choosing to carry *a book* – a text full of written words. This clasping of a book, tight in hand, showed that the book was important to them. The book was precious.

Throughout history human beings have always regarded books as something of great value. Books indeed are 'rare and beautiful treasures' (Prov. 24:4), which is why it's sometimes said that there's more bounty in finding a good book than in discovering a pot of gold. Some go further, considering books to be not just valuable, but intrinsic to humanity, with Argentine anthologist and essayist Alberto Manguel saying that 'the art of reading, in its broadest sense, defines our species'.[4] Oppressive and totalitarian regimes have understood this, not only seeking to control what people read but often encouraging the public burning of books which they deem unsuitable and subversive, and these have ranged from political books to religious writings.

Like many, the idea of forced burning of books repels me. This doesn't mean that every book is a good book, it just means that writing deserves to be heard. Some suggest that corporate book-burning is supported in the Christian tradition in Acts 19:19, which is a Bible passage recounting new converts in Ephesus, where: 'A number who had practised sorcery brought their scrolls together and burned them publicly.' The scrolls described there may have been religious books, but are more likely to have been small rolled-up scripts of magical formulas often inscribed with incantational material and curses, and held within personal jewellery such as an amulet or ankle charm. It seems that the destruction of these texts was the voluntary decision of the owner, not material being censored by authorities or a mob, and that this was a particular response by some newly converted people, signifying their break from the past and their new identity in Christ. All this means that Acts 19:19 should not be used as a justification by Christians, or any other groups, to burn books.[5] In any event, such destruction surely shouts the opposite message – of their intrinsic value, and is a recognition that we're changed by what we read and take into our lives. That's why if you want to be transformed, become a person who reads – and who reads well.

Some people, despite seeing that books are important, just struggle to read. It could be that they've never been encouraged to read. If that's you, I hope a book like this spurs you to read more. It could be they just find reading difficult. The answer for most is to practice, unless you have a medical condition like dyslexia or the inattentive kind of ADHD, where audiobooks might suit you better. Or, as author J.K. Rowling says, it might simply be: 'If you don't like to read, you haven't found the right book.'[6] If that's the case, make your way to a bookshop and step inside.

Have you ever walked into a bookshop full of books and felt overwhelmed? I have. Sometimes I enter and find it hard to know where to start. It's not that there's a shortage of books; quite the opposite – there are *too many*! The choice is indeed vast and grows every year, with about a million new titles published annually across the globe. In a world of so many books, what should I read, and where should I start?

Curiosity

I begin with a book that sparks curiosity. Rod Judkins is quite right when he says that 'The future belongs to the curious' as it 'fills us with wonder and the urge to search'.[7] That's why unless you *must* read a book, perhaps for a test of some sort, most book experts would warn you away from reading something forced on you, or something you find boring. I agree. After all, it's such hard work having to read something you just don't want to read. Instead, find something that really interests you – that stirs you, and makes you want to dig deeper. So start with a book that makes you curious.

Cover

It's the cover that's often the first thing that stands out. It might be colourful, creative or clever, or perhaps clean and simple. The designs on the front – the picture or the graphic design and the text font – catches our eye. I know that doesn't guarantee a good book, but it gets my attention. Good publishers understand this, which is why much time and thought these days goes into the look of a book.

Sometimes it's the title that draws me. A good title woos us to open up and want to find out more.

Sometimes it's the size or shape of the book that draws me in. When it's unusual, perhaps a non-standard size, it often stands out from others and I'm intrigued. I want to pick it up and discover what awaits within.

It might be the feel that I like. It could have an embossed front, or the hardback cover might be textured and feel good to touch. As I pick it up its weight could intrigue me, or perhaps I notice it sits well in my hand.

Occasionally it's the smell that captures my attention. Some new books have that distinctive 'new book' aroma which is a mix of glues and inks. Secondhand-books often smell more: perhaps it's the scent of a leather cover, but more likely it's the biscuity or even vanilla-type smell that comes from ageing, as the chemical compounds used in paper break down.[8] Our senses are more important than we realise in selecting a book.

You might choose a book because of the subject matter or the reputation of the author. Perhaps you've read something by them before, or maybe someone has recommended their writing, or you've read about them in a review. But most of the time, when browsing, I choose a book because some-thing about it or in it, is engaging. It's created interest and I'm inquisitive. I've not decided yet if I'm going to read it, but I want to find out more. So I pick it up and begin to explore.

Blurb

After glancing at the cover, I will turn the book over and read the blurb on the back or, if it's a hardback and there's a fly cover, I particularly take note of what's written there about the book at the front and the author at the back. I'll glance at the endorsements. I'll probably look at the chapter headings in the Contents page. Then I'll have a quick flick through, perhaps taking note of the start or finish of a chapter. Often a short scan like this can be done in less than a minute. If it's not a novel, there's one more impor-tant thing I do: I look to see if it has an Index at the back.

If it does, I might linger longer, noticing what and who is mentioned there, as that will help me see further things covered in the book, and who has influenced the author.[9] Indexes are a helpful and highly underrated section of a book. If after this it doesn't make me want to read more, I put it down and move on.

If you grew up around books, you may have learned to do this kind of thing when you picked up a book at home, or at school, but if not, I'd urge you to develop the habit. Do it in bookshops, in libraries and basically anywhere where there are books. I do this sometimes when I'm visiting someone's house. A book gets my attention and I'll ask if I can have a look. As well as creating an opportunity for later conversation, simply taking a few moments to be observant in this way is smart and sagacious.

If you're fairly new to reading, don't wait for a book to jump into your hand. Instead, be proactive, go looking and select something that looks interesting. That's also the view of author Philip Pullman, who advises: 'There's no such thing as a perfect book, really. You have to take a chance.'[10] So the most important thing is to begin. Just start reading. Find something – a book that sounds interesting – and begin. If you've not found what seems to be the ideal book, then don't worry. Do the best with what you've got in front of you. Make a start.

Subject

Over time most people find that certain types of books interest them. It could be a particular genre – like *fiction*, *poetry*, or *business*. For example, over the last few years I've become especially interested in *non-fiction* genre and I find myself often drawn to that section in a bookshop. As a follower of Jesus I'm particularly interested in books on different aspects of *discipleship* and *mission*, and I also read quite broadly in the field of *leadership*. It could be that you come to enjoy a particular subject, like *history*, *science fiction*, *prayer*, or *travel*. If that's the case, look out for signposts in bookshops to those subject areas. You may develop a taste for a particular aspect of a subject, like the history of the English Civil War, or female prayer leaders, or Portuguese travel books. It could be you find there's a certain author that you appreciate, and you want to devour everything they write. When it comes to *fiction*, I like reading works by the Irish author Niall Williams, and the American novelist Elizabeth Strout, so I'm always on the lookout when either of them has written something new. I like a good novel, recognising, with William Boyd, prose fiction's 'innate, subtle, wonderfully complex and effortless ability to give us [the] possibility of experiencing the inner life of others'.[11] Novels help us understand people, which can be enriching but also challenging. I've found this, especially when a character I like does something out of character. I also realise that as I've got older, my reading interests have developed and changed. That's fine. That's why I encourage people to read what they enjoy.

When choosing a book on a subject in which I'm interested, I've found it good to ask myself if I'm reading simply to justify what I already think, or to stretch my thinking. I do this because while it's fine to read things that strengthen my opinions, if I *only* do that, and don't engage with differing views, I can become rather narrow and I won't grow or learn as much as I could. Neither will I be able to engage in constructive dialogue with those who see things differently. That's why many advise us to read broadly, and to observe, especially when reading *non-fiction*, how the authors we're reading have engaged with opposing views. We might ask: have they quoted accurately and politely, or have they parodied the other's position? I also like to see if the writer ever reveals that they've changed their minds on something. That's because I want to learn from other learners. If they've changed or expanded or adjusted their view, or at least have a greater appreciation of a differing perspective, that is not only respectful; it's also healthy and wise.

Cost

Some people fail to learn through reading as they're put off by the cost of books. This is especially the case for people in poverty. Aware of this, many publishers have tried to keep prices low. For example, Allen Lane, founder of Penguin books in 1935, worked hard to ensure that each paperback cost the same as a packet of cigarettes, seeking to make it affordable for the ordinary person. Nevertheless, for some the cost of purchasing books is prohibitive to reading. This is one of the main reasons why public libraries were established, and is a good reason why they should remain a funding priority for local governments. The town library where I presently live, in Bolton, is excellent, and is a fine example of a well-resourced and attractively laid out space, which encourages reading. Bolton Council also provides a book delivery service for those who have difficulties getting to a library, or for people in residential care homes. In many areas where people live far from public libraries, councils also run mobile libraries which visit villages where books can be exchanged, and particular books ordered for future reading. Libraries are a wonderful gift to any community and should be widely celebrated, but they are often threatened with closure as part of local spending cuts. This should be resisted, for libraries are a fantastic resource, offering free reading for all. Journalist Caitlin Moran recognised this in 2011, famously describing libraries to be 'cathedrals of the mind; hospitals of the soul; theme parks of the imagination. On a cold, rainy island, they are the only sheltered public spaces where you are not a consumer, but a citizen instead. A human with a brain and a heart and a desire to be uplifted, rather than a customer with a credit card'.[12] This is why so many, including Rabbi Jonathan Sacks, have seen libraries as 'an essential element of a good society'[13] for they help us learn the art of reading.

While I'm a big fan of libraries, their only downside is that books taken out must be returned. Really, they must. They're not yours to keep for they are a shared resource. However, as I will argue in this book, it's good to own books and to develop your own mini library, if you can. I recognise this might be difficult for people on a low income, but it's not impossible. While many new books are expensive, bookstores often have sales, especially after Christmas and in the summer, when books are often well marked down. It's also good to scout secondhand bookshops and charity shops. Lots of my most cherished books are pre-used, with some having cost the price of a cup of coffee or less. Some people particularly like secondhand books, especially if there's a name inside, for that itself tells a story, of which the new owner is now becoming a part.

Even if you can only afford a few books at home, I advise people not to lock them away in a cupboard but to have some visible. This is not to show off, but for children and anyone and everyone to pick up and read. I didn't realise it at the time, but I was brought up in that kind of home, where books were present, and I am grateful. Creating an environment where reading is encouraged and where books lie around for the inquisitive to enquire, is so important. My wife, Sam, and I have tried to do that in our home, with most rooms having at least a few books in them, as we want to encourage a culture of reading in our household. Doing this doesn't have to cost a huge amount.

Opportunity

With so many books out there that I *could* read, I've become increasingly choosy about what I *do* read. Most of us know that as we read, books speak into our lives and the very situations we're living in. As I'm a prayerful person I ask the Spirit of God to guide me to a helpful book for this moment in my life, so I am reading things that will be pertinent to my life and work. I might pray this not only as part of my regular prayers but more spontaneously, under my breath, as I walk into a bookshop. I advise other readers to do the same. It might be a book that energises or inspires me, or gives me fresh joy, or stretches my imagination. It could be a book that gives me tools to use in various contexts – like in the workplace, or at home, for example in my parenting. It's good to be informed, but I'm also wanting to be *formed*. I'm seeking to digest a good and healthy diet of reading over time that will help me grow as a human being who's a missionary follower of Jesus.

If you're not someone who follows Christ or prays, I'd still advise that you look out for a timely book – that is, a book that's relevant to your life right now.[14] Secular writer

Alberto Manguel concurs, saying that 'certain books are right for certain occasions'.[15] So be observant of what's out there in the hope of finding a helpful book for the season of life that you're in. Here are three ways that I do this.

One is by regularly going into bookshops. I do this even if I have no intention to buy. I like to see what's in stock and what people are writing, taking particular note of the *New Releases* section, as well as the *Manager's* or *Staff Recommendations*. Sometimes bookshop staff leave a little personal note next to a book saying why they like it. I love reading those.

The second is by using the media. There are many online resources to helps us, with all sorts of websites recommending books. Some use social media sites such as *Booktok* on TikTok. I sometimes listen to podcasts from Penguin and *The New York Times Literary Review*, where reviewers recommend books they like. I also enjoy looking at the *Book Review* section in a weekly newspaper. Most of the broadsheets highlight choice books, and so when I buy a weekend paper I like to flick through and see what's being recommended and reviewed. If something looks interesting, I may cut out the review and put it in my wallet, or take a photo/screenshot on my phone, which then helps me when I'm browsing online or in a bookshop.

Third, when I find an author I like, I will often find out who *their* favourite authors are. I want to know who's influenced them, and I may want to follow that up by reading what they've read. If the book has References and a Bibliography and/or Index, you can find out much from there. If it's a novel, you can discover their influences from an internet search of the author, where there'll probably be some articles and blogs by them or about them. If you're willing to follow the trail, it often opens up into a new and intriguing landscape of discovery.

So when it comes to choosing a book, I seek to be ready and expectant.[16] What's most important is to be on the lookout, proactively searching for a text that's interesting and helpful for your life at that time.

Transformation

When I read I want my vision to be transformed. I desire to grow. To learn. To understand. I want to enter the world of the writer and enjoy a journey of exploration and be changed. I do this both for myself and for others – so I can be a bringer of positive change through my life.

This potential for growth and change is greater if you can fluently read more than one language. Being bi- or multi-lingual will allow you to read particularly broadly, enjoying all sorts of books that are only available in the language of their author. After all, few books get translated into multiple languages. For example, if you can read Mandarin, Spanish and Arabic as well as English, a myriad of authors and texts is open to you – books that people like me, who can only read English, will never be able to access and appreciate. However, it's worth remembering that if you really want to be transformed through your reading, it's best to read in your *heart language*.

Your heart language is the language you speak at home. It's the language with which you address parents and close family. It's the language in which you pray. For many, particularly in African, Asian and South American contexts, this may well be a local language or dialect, rather than the main national language. Bible translators especially understand this, which is why they are keen to ensure the Bible is translated into as many local languages as possible. I write about this in *A–Z of Prayer*,[17] noting that it's speaking and reading in the heart language which tends to produce spiritual transformation, generating conversion and significant spiritual growth. Such change is not, however, limited to spiritual growth, but to every aspect of life, with evidence showing that when we read and hear in our heart language our emotions are particularly stimulated, which often results in positive learning and development.[18] So for any polyglots – that is, people who can understand two or more languages – enjoy accessing a breadth of reading, but recognise that when reading with a vision for transformation, it's best to choose a book written in your heart language.

Sometimes I will pick up a novel which someone has recommended, and I begin reading. It might spark curiosity with interesting characters and perhaps an intriguing storyline. I may enjoy the reading as far as it goes, but I soon recognise it's not a classic and it's not impacting my life. That's OK. While I want to grow from my reading, there's nothing wrong with reading a book that soon gets forgotten. It has some satisfaction, filling a gap for a while, rather like eating fast-food. But like fast-food, it won't satisfy for long and isn't sufficient for a healthy life. Reading that kind of book can feel like watching a B movie, which is fine as far is it goes, but I'll probably forget both the name of the film and its plot by tomorrow. But the difference of course is that reading a book takes a lot longer than a ten-minute Big Mac or watching a 100-minute film – and time is limited. So I tend not to read too many 'average' books. I try, if possible, to read more discerningly.

What about not finishing a book?[19] People often get concerned about that, especially if they've spent good money on a book, or perhaps been given it as a special gift. Is it OK not to finish? The short answer is *yes*. While sometimes we should persevere with a book, I normally advise that if it isn't keeping your attention, put it down. You can always come back to it. I do this quite often, sometimes coming back to a book that I got partway through some months ago. At other times I stop simply because I'm distracted by another that seems more interesting. If the first is good, though, I will try to return to it at some point, occasionally finding when I do that it's more relevant to my life than ever, speaking into the moment in which I'm living.

Occasionally I'll find a book that's special. As I begin reading, I soon realise this is the very book I should be reading *right now.* When I began writing this book in early 2023, preparing to transition from being a local church leader to a bishop, I found a book like that. It was Rabbi Jonathan Sacks' book *Lessons in Leadership*[20] based on the Torah, the first five books of the Bible, and it was a delight to read his wise reflections on inspiring sacred texts and hear his application to contemporary life and leadership. It felt like a prophetic moment for me. When I find such a book, my mind is stimulated and my heart stirred. As I read on, I know I'm on a journey of renewal and I often long that the book would go on and on forever. Books like that are rare but important, and they become very precious to us. Twentieth-century English scholar and acclaimed writer C.S. Lewis, who penned the Narnia series, found such a book as he read *Phantastes* by George MacDonald when he was a young man. 'That night' he later wrote, 'my imagination was, in a certain sense, baptised; the rest of me, not unnaturally, took longer.'[21] Lewis knew he would never be the same again.

Not all books will change your life like that. Alberto Manguel agrees, saying that 'Not every book is an epiphany' but nevertheless we can still be navigated 'by a luminous page or a beacon of verse'.[22] As I journey through life, I hope that most of the books I read will help me in some way, for I want to be nourished and fed. Sometimes I want to be entertained. Sometimes I want practical advice. Sometimes I'm not sure what I want, but I realise I'm just enjoying the book. Occasionally I might find myself identifying with certain things in a book, and it begins to feel like some or even all the words are written *just for me*. Perhaps I now see something in my life in a whole new light. Or the book reveals exactly what I'm thinking or feeling, expressing what to date I've found hard to put in words. Or I feel challenged in my thinking or my actions. Or I closely identify with a particular character and their experience starts to become mine. Or I understand something I've never before grasped. Or a fresh line of thinking opens up. Or the book helps me with exactly the issues I'm facing. If I find a book like that, it feels like an opportune moment and I cherish it. I am thankful. I dive in and immerse myself in it, excited by what it will do in me and for me. That's because I'm reading with a vision for transformation.

You can't read everything, so choose books carefully. Make the most of what you read, recognising that not every book will change your life, but some will. So don't just read any old thing. Instead, choose books judiciously, being curious about what you read.

For some people, choosing a book is the hardest bit. They procrastinate and end up reading nothing. Don't do that. Look for a book. Pray for a book. Seek for a book. Find a book. And take it home to read.

- pick up books regularly and enjoy taking a look

- read books that sparks curiosity

- pray about what you read

- welcome books that speak into your life

- read with a vision for transformation

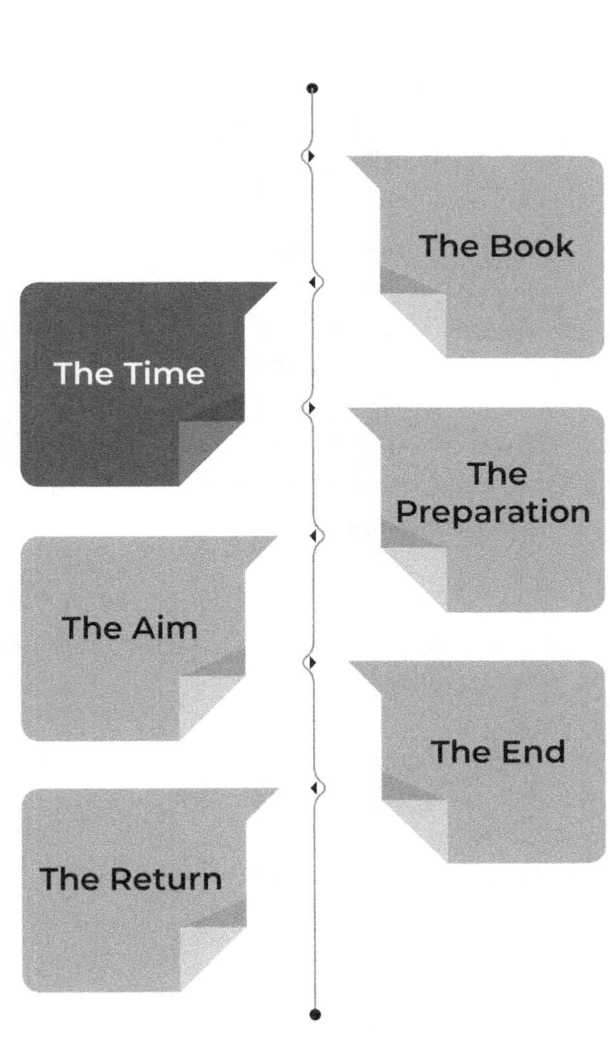
The Book
The Time
The Preparation
The Aim
The End
The Return

Chapter 2

Plan with care

- 'There is a time for everything, and a season for every activity under the heavens' (Eccl. 3:1).

- 'No matter how busy you may think you are, you must find time for reading, or surrender yourself to self-chosen ignorance' (Confucius).[1]

- 'They say that time is money, but that's not true. Time is life. And if I want the fullest life, I need to find fullest time' (Ann Voskamp).[2]

- 'We do have enough time. Life is long, if we listen to ourselves often enough, and look up' (Erling Kagge).[3]

Once you have a book to read, you need to find the time to read it.

Just occasionally I find a book that I just can't put down. I start to read, and it's *so* good, *so* gripping, *so* glorious that every spare minute of every day is used up reading it. That means it gets read quickly.

It was like that when I began to read Walter Isaacson's biography of Steve Jobs in late 2011.[4] I had preordered it and it arrived in the post at the start of a very busy week for me, but somehow I managed to read its 656 pages in just a few days. It was brilliantly written in Isaacson's journalistic style but most importantly Jobs just fascinated me, and by reading the book I felt I learned so much about this most intriguing person.[5] Normally though, I can't read so many pages in a few days. I have a wife and family with whom I share my life, and I have a demanding full-time job. I mustn't neglect my primary responsibilities. And yet I know that reading equips and empowers me, so I must carve out time and space for it. So how can I do that?

There's no one way to find time. The main thing is to be intentional. But you will only be intentional if you're convinced that reading is important.

Benefits

If you've picked up this book, and come this far, I trust you're starting to become convinced that reading is valuable. But if you need more persuading, here are nine particular reasons why reading is beneficial:

1. *Reading can increase knowledge*
   Many read to learn. Reading educates and informs us, giving us knowledge about history, ideas, culture and the world.[6]
2. *Reading can develop the imagination*
   Reading is one of the main ways we grow in thoughtfulness, inventiveness and artistry.[7]
3. *Reading can develop many skills, including communication skills*
   Many find they are better at speaking, writing and conversing, through reading.[8]
4. *Reading can enhance emotional intelligence, especially empathy*
   We learn much about people through reading. Novels, for example, help us to access people's minds and hearts.[9]
5. *Reading can grow character*
   Many testify to growing in virtues, through reading.[10]
6. *Reading can entertain*
   Lots of people read as a hobby and as a means of delight and distraction.[11]
7. *Reading can relax us and comfort us, being good for mental health*
   Many unwind and find solace as they read.[12]
8. *Reading can make us more interesting people*
   Reading opens the door to a whole world of story and adventure, that stretches and broadens our awareness and insight.[13]

9. *Reading can transform us into people of influence*
   Reading often empowers people to bring positive change to the world.[14]

This list should assure readers that spending time reading is time very well spent. So why then do so many people find it hard to make time to read? One of the main reasons is that reading is *important*, but not *urgent*.

Eisenhower

In the world of time management, those who want to grasp the difference between what's important and what's urgent have been helped by the *Eisenhower Matrix*, sometimes known as the 4-quadrant *Important-Urgent Matrix*, and named after the thirty-fourth president of the United States, Dwight Eisenhower. It looks like this:

	URGENT	NOT URGENT
IMPORTANT	Quadrant I: *Urgent & Important*	Quadrant II: *Not Urgent & Important*
NOT IMPORTANT	Quadrant III: *Urgent & Not Important*	Quadrant IV: *Not Urgent & Not Important*

If something is 'Not Urgent and Not Important' (Q IV) then I do my best to avoid it – I'm usually wasting my time. If something is the opposite, that is 'Urgent and Important' (Q I), then I should drop everything and do it right now! Next is a matter which is 'Urgent and Not Important' (Q III); most of us hope there aren't too many jobs like that as they feel like a bad use of time. Finally, some tasks in life are 'Not Urgent and Important' (Q II). These are things that are easily and often pushed out by more pressing things. But we neglect them at our peril. They don't need doing immediately, so often we don't do them, or we put them off. But if we keep avoiding them, we'll be in trouble. Keeping fit is a good personal example. In the workplace, training and developing leaders would be another. These are Q II tasks – important but not urgent. They often don't happen because we get distracted by matters that demand our immediate attention. But if we're willing to be disciplined and make time and do these things, then there will, over time, be immense benefit.

Reading is a Q II task. I'm convinced of it. We've just taken note of nine benefits of reading, recognising that reading helps us grow, especially in character and influence. It's good for us and for others. So it *is* important, but it's rarely *urgent*. That means unless I prioritise it, it'll get pushed out by other more demanding things. Therefore I must make space in my life for reading. It's important. It really is.

When you're convinced of this, you will want to make time for reading. Here's how I do it.

Morning

When I wake up, I go downstairs, make some tea and go into my study. I then spend time in prayer and quiet reading. I read the Bible and reflect on its message. In doing this, I'm following in a long tradition of women and men who've done the same. John Wesley, founder of the Methodist movement in the eighteenth century, stands out as a particularly helpful guide. He said: 'Read and pray daily. It is for your life. There is no other way.'[15] I've been doing this for over forty years, morning after morning after morning – and it's the best start to the day. I love it! I do this not just because I am a church leader, but because I'm seeking wisdom as a follower of Jesus. It's one way of ensuring the Bible gets into me, and is the first thing I read each day. I do this because I consider the Bible to be the 'Book of books'.[16] Often I will end this first part of the day with further reading from a devotional book that intentionally feeds my soul, and sometimes I will journal too.

If you're not a person of faith, I'd still urge you to start your day with reading. If you don't read from the Bible, read something inspirational.[17] To begin each day with words that comfort or challenge and encourage or equip is a healthy thing to do. In fact there's good scientific research to show that this is beneficial for our emotional and psychological wellbeing.[18] Human history is littered with examples of people who've done this over the years, and found it to be highly motivational, releasing energy, ideas and productivity for the day ahead. According to Alex Soojung-Kim Pang, 'Many notable creatives do their most intense work early in the morning, when their minds are freshest and least prone to distraction.'[19] Try it, and discover with me, that the mornings are made for reading.

Free

Many of us think we don't have any free time to read in our day, but if we step back and consider things, actually most of us do. The average person works about forty hours a week and sleeps fifty-six hours a week (i.e. eight hours per night), which potentially leaves a huge 112 hours in the week. I know most of us have many things to do in those remaining hours, but if we stop and look honestly at our diaries, we probably can find *some* time each week to read – even one hour – if we really want to. It's simply a matter of prioritising and practising.

If your week looks incredibly busy, then how about using your lunchbreak at work? Or making the most of the commute to work, perhaps on a bus or train? There normally is time, if we search for it. That's why I advise people, if they can, to have a book in their bag, or something to read on their Kindle or tablet, or an audiobook downloaded on their phone. That's what I do. Then I'm ready to read whenever I have a few minutes.

Dead

There's also time in each day when I can read while doing something else. This is about multitasking. I can read a book while sitting on the loo or taking a bath. I can have an audiobook on headphones while at the gym or taking other forms of daily exercise. These periods of what's sometimes called *dead time*, over a week and a month, all add up. If you can learn to use some of this dead time to read, you'll be surprised how much reading you can do.

Bed

Some of us are exhausted by bedtime. That's normally the case for me, so I don't want a heavy book by my bed to stretch my thinking before I sleep. Instead, I have something more lightweight or gently thoughtful to reflect on, before my wife and I pray and sleep. I recall in 2020 I enjoyed reading Erling Kagge's book on *Walking*[20] before I went to sleep. I found it an excellent bedside book and I enjoyed dipping into it most evenings for a few minutes. By reading this way I finished it in just a few weeks.

Holidays

Holidays are a great time to read, but care needs to be taken. Most of us use holidays to change our pace of life and enjoy space outside of normal routine. They're times to travel, to sleep, to rejuvenate and be renewed. If we holiday with others, they're also times to reconnect with loved ones, investing in family and friends. This means if you're a book lover, take care not to neglect those key relationships. If I have my head in a book from the moment I go on holiday until the day I arrive back in the office, then I might have had my imagination revived but my spouse will feel neglected and my kids distant. So reading on holiday requires good communication – even negotiation – unless you go away on your own.

Assuming such negotiations are agreed and kept to, then I'd advise you read to your heart's content. Think what you'd like to read beforehand, and prepare well. I often save up a few books, ready to be read when on holiday. If you're on holiday for a week, you'll probably find you can read a number of books during that time. That can make holidays incredibly enriching, wherever you go. When away I often talk with those around me about what I and they are reading. At mealtimes and other times, we share our insights, questions and reflections. Holidays can be times of much shared resourcing and reading. Two of you might even want to read the same book at the same time, and then share your discoveries.

Bravery

In some subcultures down the ages, reading has been discouraged. This was often the case in the past in the UK where some agricultural or working-class communities considered reading to be a genteel pastime for the middle or upper class, viewing it as an interference from the real, day-to-day struggles of getting by and earning a living. This was especially so in contexts where literacy was low and only the wealthy elite were encouraged to read. Often this resulted in young people from more deprived backgrounds having to read in secret, for fear of being teased at home or school. To push past this social pressure required determination and bravery, with books having to be hidden. This can still happen today in various forms, especially in non-book cultures, such as urban housing estates. Some want their children to develop what they see as purely practical skills, viewing reading as a hobby for intellectuals. But the wise will urge those around them to read, knowing that reading is always good and incredibly useful, expanding the mind and opening the heart, sparking imagination and preparing us well for a life of ongoing work and learning.

I realise that finding time to read, when life is busy and work is hard, can seem like an impossible luxury. This is how some feel who are working all hours to survive and keep food on the table. The idea of catching just a few minutes to read, never mind being able to afford a holiday for reading, seems unattainable. This is why we need to recognise that books are lifegiving and resourcing, and do all we can to find a good book and eke out some time for reading. Those who do this often discover that rather than being an unhelpful addition to the demands of life, books actually equip and encourage us in the daily grind. As we've seen, reading is not urgent, but it *is* important. Schools model this well when they prioritise storytime at the end of the school day, with many classes creating timetable space for children to gather and sit together while the teacher reads a story. There are many authors today, especially who grew up in poor households, who say that it was school storytime that created a love of books. Creating a safe and happy environment where reading is encouraged can be truly transformational.

One of my roles as a bishop in Manchester is to oversee local prison and probation ministry, so from time to time I visit prisons. Normally there's some time to look around and meet inmates. I often notice those who are reading. They may be in their cell, but they may be in a class or on a computer, learning a new skill or taking a course. They know that reading opens a door of opportunity for them, not just to escape from reality but to be empowered to start a new life. I admire their courage.

Variety

To help me be empowered through reading, I invariably have a number of books on the go at one time. There's nothing wrong with reading more than one book at once. Indeed, it helps me enjoy a rich and broad literary diet. While it's good in life to have a few areas of specialism, it's helpful to be eclectic and read widely. There's increasing evidence that it is people who are *broad* rather than *deep* (i.e. having a breadth of knowledge and experience, rather than being deep specialists in just one or two fields), who are best able to offer the wise, creative, adaptive kind of leadership required in today's complex world.[21] So I often have two or three books on the go at once, often covering different subjects – maybe a Christian devotional book, a book about architecture and a travel book. I tend to have one book which I read in the mornings, and another at night. I might carry another with me, to read in gaps when I'm out and about. I might save up a book to read when I'm in a different context (e.g. on retreat, or on holiday). But I rarely have more than three books on the go at once, as the ideas or plots start to get mixed up in my mind, and I soon find myself confused.

Intentionality

As we get older, we recognise that there are periods in our lives when we have more time to read, and others when we have less. If, say, you're holding down more than one job and working all hours, or you have a young family, time is normally tight and space to read is greatly limited and so very precious. That's OK. Just make the most of the time you have. I began doing some initial research for this book during the coronavirus pandemic of 2020/21. It was a sad season for many, with loved ones dying and NHS staff and other key workers giving their all to serve people. I was busy myself, working from home, caring for our church and wider community online and via phone calls, texts and Zoom calls. But by being intentional I was able to carve out some time each day for reading, reflecting and writing. Crises always create opportunities.

If you just can't find the opportunity to read but you want to, why not find creative ways to be prompted? Here are two things you could do. One is to tell a friend that you want to read more, and ask them to nag you about it. This can be more helpful than you think. The other is to journal about it. I talk more about journalling in Chapter 5, and have written a whole book about it as part of this *Art of . . .* series, because journalling is important in helping us become more reflective. So why not journal about wanting to read more? Write down your hopes and desires and intentions. And then re-read your journal regularly. You'll soon see if you've responded to your musings. And then journal again about it, and about how you're doing. The entries don't need to be long, they just need to be honest. For some, journalling about reading may be the tool that gets you reading.

When it comes to reading, do what you can in the season you're in. If your life is demanding and busy, then be purposeful, and use your dead time well. There *is* time to read. You just have to go looking for it. As you find it, I suspect you'll discover that you have more time to read than you think.

- be convinced that reading is important

- use the mornings and holidays

- read intentionally during 'free' time

- aim for a good broad diet of reading

- don't read too many books at once

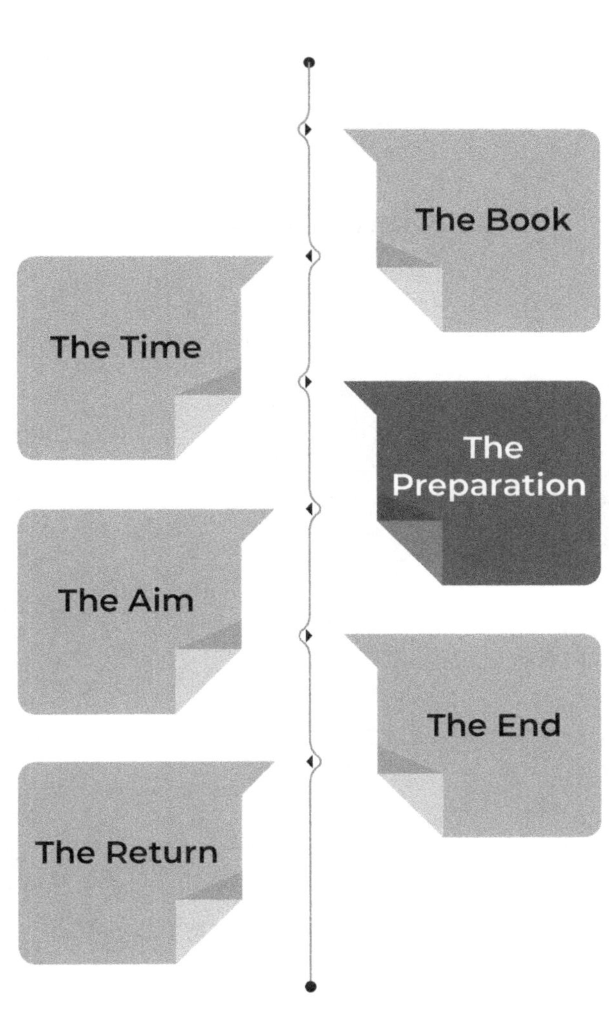

The Time
The Aim
The Return
The Book
The Preparation
The End

Chapter 3

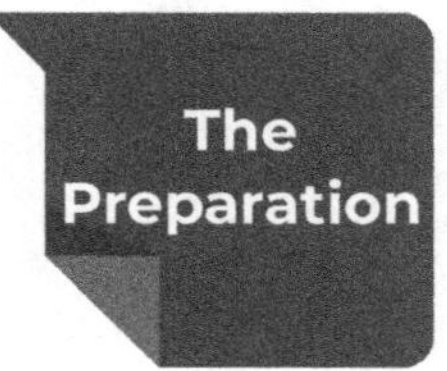

Approach with attentiveness

- *'We must pay the most careful attention, therefore, to what we have heard, so that we do not drift away'* (Heb. 2:1).

- *'The practice of paying attention awakens us to what is extraordinary in the midst of the ordinary'* (Ruth Haley Barton).[1]

- *'distraction remains a destroyer of depth'* (Cal Newport).[2]

- *'Are you prepared for what God is preparing?'* (Randy Clark).[3]

I used to think that reading just involved picking up a book and sitting down to read. Then I heard Rick Warren's talk on 'How to Read' and I changed my ways.

Pencil

Warren could not have been clearer when he said that the key to good reading is to read with a pencil. Those might not have been his exact words, but I know it's what he meant. He urged his listeners to have a pencil nearby and to write in the books you read. Since hearing those words I've discovered that others agree, including avid reader and author Mark Batterson, who says: 'I won't even open a book if I don't have a pen to underline with.'[4]

At first I wasn't sure about the pen/pencil thing. I'd read and enjoyed quite a few books without needing to have a writing implement at hand. In fact I'd only written inside a book in pencil when studying at school or university, and I didn't really want all my reading to always feel like an academic exercise, so I initially rejected this advice.

The other thing that it took me a while to recognise and acknowledge was that I actually felt deeply uncomfortable about scribbling in books, seeing it as violating them. This was partly because I saw books as important and valuable, but also because teachers at my primary school used to admonish anyone and everyone for writing in books. They'd called it 'defacing' and it no doubt influenced me to always want books to remain clean and tidy. I didn't really realise this reticence to use a pencil at the time, but looking back now, I can see it. To underline, draw, scribble or write personal comments on, or in, a book felt like vandalism.

Until I did it.

I reluctantly forced myself to try Warren's technique. I pushed past my concerns and found a pencil and started marking up my books. Once I did it, I knew Warren was right. And now I can say with clarity and conviction that reading with a pencil has become a core practice that has revolutionised my reading. This has become so important to me that I normally carry a pencil with me on all occasions, so I'm ready to read.

I can't remember if Warren gave advice on what to do with the pencil. So, having used a pencil for well over twenty-five years now, here's what I do.

When I read something that stands out, I underline it in pencil. It might be a phrase that seems important to the book. It might be an insight that I find interesting. It might be a definition. It might be a key comment from a character that changes the direction of the book. It might be an observation into human nature that makes me think. Basically it can be anything. Also if a key word is significant to the text, perhaps reflecting an important theme in the book, I will circle it. I then scribble something in the margin next to my underlinings and circlings. It's usually just a few words, summarising what I'm marking. So most of my books now have underlinings and circles in the text, and notes in the margins. The only exceptions are a few very old, irreplaceable books, that I choose not to mark up because of their historicity or value.

I've found that using a pencil in this way really helps me with my reading. Research shows that writing things down aids the memory[5] and provides a useful record, enabling us to go back and take account of the matters we've been considering. It explains why teachers and tutors often advise students to take notes, and also, tellingly, why twentieth-century Soviet dictator Joseph Stalin did not want meetings recorded and would not allow his Politburo members to take notes.[6] Interestingly, writing and reading use different parts of the brain, so when we pause and underline and scribble a note, we're stretching our minds which leads to a richer memory. That's why it's normally good to take notes if we want to learn and become wiser.

My scribblings also provide reference points through the book. They're like personal markers or flags. Sometimes if I pick up a book I've not read for a few days or even weeks, I will flick back to my pencil markings, to remind myself of a few things. Not only do they help me see where I've got up to, but they remind me of what's been covered. These pencil notes are also important when I finish a book – but more on that later.

The other thing that I've started doing with my pencil as I read these days, is write summary notes. I don't do this with every book, but when I do, it's almost always helpful, especially if I return to the book later. Let me explain how this works.

When I come to the end of a chapter – especially if it's, say, a *non-fiction* book with a cumulative argument – I might go back to the beginning of the chapter and write in pencil, on the chapter page, the core theme or ideas in that chapter. This forces me to think back about what I've just read to check that I've understood it. If I can't summarise it in a few words or bullet points, I've probably not grasped what's being said. Sometimes I will do this not just for a chapter, but for the whole book. So in one of those blank spaces perhaps near the inside cover, I'll scribble some of the key themes of the entire book, and perhaps a page number that summarises it well. That way, if or when I come back to the book, I can flick through and quickly be reminded of the key ideas and where to find them in the future. If I return to a book marked like this, reading this summary page takes a lot less time than looking through and reading my margin notes.

I was having breakfast with my friend Gary recently. Having been a prolific reader for some time he was telling me how he now wants to get more out of his reading, and that he's decided that the main way he's going to do this is by intentionally marking up his books. He now does this more than ever: underlining, taking notes and pausing to scribble summaries of what he's read. This, he says, helps him take things in better, so that he can be more effectively shaped and changed by what he reads. I am delighted.

C.S. Lewis's gathered writings about reading, entitled *The Reading Life*, show that Lewis did something not dissimilar. He said:

> To enjoy a book … I begin by making a map on one end of the leafs: then I put in a genealogical tree or two. Then I put a running headline at the top of each page: finally I index at the end all the passages I have for any reason underlined. I often wonder – considering how people enjoy themselves developing photos or making scrapbooks – why so few people make a hobby of their reading in this way.[7]

If you've never done it before, find a noting system that works for you, and in particular use a pencil.

A simple, cheap, inexpensive pencil will do, perhaps with a rubber on the end. A good thing about this key reading resource of a pencil is that it doesn't cost much. It's not just for the rich, but for all. It's easy to use and has stood the test of time. While the commercial pencil was invented by Nicholas-Jacques Conte in 1785 and the first factory opened in Cumberland in 1832, pencil-type writing implements have been around for many years, and will continue to be. They're so simple and useful. Sometimes I just grab whatever pencil I can find, but if I can I'll use my favourite pencil – a Kerry mechanical pencil, which is the pencil of choice for many architects. It's the pencil I normally carry with me.[8] In the end, though, any pencil will do. Just find one that works and keep it next to the book you're reading.

Distractions

When I'm ready, I sit down with my book, with my Kerry pencil close by, and I start to read. However I know that I am easily distracted from reading. Social media is everywhere, and emails and texts are constantly pummelling us. So I have to push those things to one side if I'm going to read – even for just a few minutes. Some of us will find this harder than others. If that's you, be deliberate. Go to a different room or space, leave your computer or phone behind, and find a chair or somewhere comfortable to be. Maybe sit on the loo. Or go and stand outside. My son Joel puts on his noise-cancelling headphones. What's important is to find a space with few distractions so you're ready to read.[9]

Having no or minimal interruptions enables the reader to read with focus and intent. But this is not easy. Writing in the pre-digital days of 1854, Henry David Thoreau in

Walden knew this, saying that 'books must be read as deliberately as they were written'.[10] He knew that we get the most out of reading when we make space, purposefully prepare, and stay focused. In these days of smartphone instant connection, creating space to concentrate on the book in hand can be difficult. The only way to do this is to be disciplined. Neglect the multiple voices demanding your attention through your phone and deliberately chose the one voice speaking through your book. Push distractions aside and start to read.

While our phones bring a number of benefits to life in the early twenty-first century, there's growing evidence today of their detrimental effect to much of life, with social media, chatrooms and online pornography greatly affecting people's mental and emotional health, creating insecurity about identity, lack of sociability and strengthening addictive behaviours. This is especially so if young people spend significant time on phones during childhood and adolescence. As Jonathan Haidt has shown in *The Anxious Generation*, there's a great need for us all, and especially children, to severely limit time on our phones.[11] Certainly replacing a phone with a book would be a sensible thing for most of us to do, especially children. One person recently who has tried to take this seriously told me how she has deleted all the social media apps on her phone, and replaced them with the Kindle app, and the result has been transformatory, resulting in much more reading and at a greater depth.

Attentiveness

I've found that if I want to read in a focused way, it's good to check myself and my disposition. If I am tired, I probably won't be able to concentrate on a heavy text. If I am anxious, I know my mind will wander, so do I need to stop and pray, or maybe call a friend, rather than read a book? I also want to acknowledge my motives for reading the text before me, checking my heart. I might ask myself: why am I reading this book? What am I anticipating? As best I can, I will want to set aside any preconceived ideas or prejudices I bring, so I can read with an alert mind and open heart.[12] If my attitude isn't right, then I'm unlikely to benefit most from the reading. I can't be attentive to the book if I'm not attentive to myself.

Being self-aware in this way includes recognising the worldview that I bring to my reading. I didn't always take note of this, but I now recognise that who I am, and my philosophy of life greatly shape the disposition I bring to reading, deeply impacting how I read. As a follower of Jesus, I am always wanting to discover, grow and change for good, so the world around me can do the same. This means I read from a place of lifelong learning. Of course, not all people approach reading in this way. Many don't ever consider the disposition they bring to reading, or indeed, to life as a whole. They just get on with things, and read whatever they fancy. While there's no shame in that, it lacks intentionality. It doesn't reflect a life of purpose – wanting to make a real difference in the world. Research shows that those with most purpose are often those with religious faith.[13] That's one of the reasons why I like to invite people to begin a relationship with God through Jesus Christ, because I know, both from my own experience and that of others, how helpful and hopeful it is to follow Jesus. Indeed, one thing that Christ-followers have, and bring, is hope for the future.[14] Ultimately this is the future hope of heaven – of life beyond the grave – but it is more than that, it is hope *now*. It is hope in and for the present.

There's so much to discover in life. Through people, through travel, through listening and reading. That's why we need to pay attention. It interests me that when author Anne Lamott is asked how she became a writer, she often says, 'My father told me to pay attention and to take notes.'[15] She wrote things down, often using a pencil – but first she took notice. She observed. She learned to live attentively.

Reading attentively, with a positive disposition of lifelong learning is, I believe, a good way to approach reading. It's what I recommend to people. It nudges and cajoles me to be strategic not just in *what* I read, but *how* I read. It causes me to read positively. Contentedly. Gladly. Joyfully. That doesn't mean that everything I read has to be deep and meaningful. I might, for example, read a message online which is frivolous and funny. That's OK – it may be just what I need at that moment and might even strengthen my ability to bring joy to others. Or I might read an appliance's instruction manual to troubleshoot an issue, and after much reading discover that it doesn't answer my question. When I fail to do that with hope, I just get annoyed and grumpy. But if I read attentively and positively, I find I'm not only more patient, but also looking for the good even in the midst of frustration. This applies particularly when reading fiction. I'm searching for the good and helpful, even if I read something difficult or painful or distressing. I'm seeking to learn, to empathise and to become more compassionate.

So I advocate that people approach their reading attentively, for lifelong learning. This would certainly be my recommendation to followers of Jesus – who should be the most hopeful people in the world – as we seek to grow and live better in God's world through reading; but this applies more broadly to all.

Inquisitive

Bringing an attentive disposition means that rather than suspending our critical faculties when we pick up a book, instead we approach each text with good questions, wanting to read with care and intent, desiring the experience to shape us. In order to do this well, thoughtful readers need to ask some inquisitive questions both *before* they read, and *as* they read.

Here are four questions I bring to my reading:

1. *Is the book reliable?*

By this, I mean: is it trustworthy? Some might similarly ask: is it true? If I'm reading *History*, or a *Biography* or *Autobiography*, I assume that the person has done their research, and it is correct, and if they're unsure about some facts, they should say so. However I've learned that some writers don't always do this, presenting ideas and theories as if they are reality. So without reading sceptically – as that doesn't aid open-mindedness – I seek to read inquisitively and will sometimes check their sources. I might look to see if the works upon which they rely seem trustworthy and whether they've used hard data from genuine archives as well as citing research from a variety of publications in a breadth of fields, perhaps from sociology and anthropology or psychology and medicine. I like to know if the author is speculating, or sharing a new hypothesis, or simply offering their opinion. Such details really help. If it's a novel, it's either a work of *fiction* which means it's a made-up story and has no factual basis, or it could be *historical fiction* so it will contain some factual events that really happened. I recognise that a fictitious novel is likely to contain some elements of the author's experience, and may reflect something they've been told by others,[16] but I don't assume their fiction describes actual past events, unless they say otherwise. I've also discovered that a good novel, like Hardy's *Tess of the D'Urbervilles*, will contain *truth*, in that it deals with real-life issues, experiences, virtues, and emotions; so there's much to discover and learn.

2. What assumptions is the author bringing to their writing?

This may not be immediately apparent, so discovering this might be part of my journey through the book. And of course I don't have to agree with, or embrace all the cultural, historical, ethical or religious assumptions of the author to enjoy it or find it helpful. But what I do need to do is to read discerningly, especially when I am presented with a particular interpretation of events.

For example, two sociology books might agree about *what* happened, but differ greatly on *why*. Historians, for example, love to include facts – such as information about people and places and dates – into their works, but these facts require selection, which will be greatly shaped by the interpretation the author brings to their work. Some books present matters as established facts, but as I dig deeper I find they are supposition or conjecture, or even speculation. This is why it's good to be curious and ask searching questions, not just of the text but also of the presumptions which the author is bringing to their writing.

Here's an example from theology. There were many theological books and Bible commentaries written in the first half of the twentieth century by academic scholars who approached the Bible with various post-Enlightenment, modernist assumptions. One was a disbelief in prophetic oracles, so they presumed that any predictive message in the biblical text which later came true was probably made up by a future editor. Another would be their understanding of miracles, that any recorded supernatural or miraculous occurrences did not actually happen. In their minds, the biblical authors probably *thought* they were miracles, but modern people, like these authors, know there must be a more reasonable explanation. However, many people today, in the twenty-first century, recognise that once someone has experienced firsthand prophetic ministry and/or miraculous occurrences – as many like me have – these rationalist cultural assumptions are undermined and often rejected. They are what scholars call an *a priori* bias. Knowing this helps me when I read a commentary with these anti-supernatural cultural assumptions. It doesn't mean they don't make some good points, or that everything they write should be rejected, but it does mean I probably won't agree with all their conclusions.

3. What is the aim of the book?

Many are interested in knowing not just what an author has written, but why. This is not always easy to discover, especially as some writers don't want to say. When it comes to *fiction*, purpose is not normally stated; the novelist simply wants you to read and experience the story. A novel's aim may be complex, and intent will very much depend on the author, with some explaining in post-publication interviews why they've written. But many don't; instead they want the reader to draw their own conclusion. In *poetry*, for example, authors sometimes tell us a theme that's inspired them, but are less clear about purpose. Writers in other fields are often more upfront about their aim, which is sometimes so in *history* and usually the case in *non-fiction*. This book, for example, explains in the Introduction why I'm writing it, and the subtitle summarises this, explaining that this book is about 'Becoming a wiser person'.

4. Will the book help me in my life?

I've found that different books will help me at different times. So I advise people to do their homework: learn how to pick up a book and find out what it's about. Does it spark interest? Is it timely? If you have time, read a section and as you read, ask yourself: do I find it hard to put it down? And here's a wise supplementary for hopeful readers: will it help me to help others?

Before I read a *non-fiction* book, I try to be inquisitive with further questions. Here are a few:

- *What is the subject of this book?*
  The title might give it away, but not always these days, as it's popular at present to have a catchy title that needs explaining – like, *Quiet* or *What the Dog Saw*. So I read the blurb. I look at the opening and closing pages. I notice how chapters end.
- *What subjects and issues does it cover?*
  I find the Contents page. And in particular, I check any Index.
- *Who is the author?*
  I look for their name. Have I heard of them? Who has endorsed them? What are their credentials, and do they have suitable background to be writing a book like this? What are their qualifications and experience? Their age? Their ethnicity? Their beliefs and passions? Their ideological (sociological, political or religious) perspectives? What is their bias, for all authors have them?[17]
- *Who are the publishers?*
  While many publishers produce books covering a breadth of subjects, I've discovered that some are more specific. So this book is published by *Authentic Media* who are a reputable Christian publishing house. They produce thoughtful books written by followers of Jesus, and on the back cover of every book Authentic are clear why

they publish books.[18] In contrast *The School of Life* publishers only produce material which is written by atheists and champion a fully secular perspective. While *Faber & Faber* publish a breadth of literature, they're especially known for good poetry. Other publishers, like Taschen, particularly produce art books. As I've grown in my reading, I've found that understanding who the publishers are can sometimes help guide my choice of reading.

- *Do they reference studies, as well as other sources and authors?*

  I look at the Notes and/or References. In the Index, I see who they are citing.

- *What audience are they speaking to?*

  Do they say who they're writing for? Authors often do this in the first few pages; it's worth taking a look. If, for example, you are British and read a book where an American author only deals with matters relevant to the United States, then it's good to know this before you read. There may be some good learning, but alternatively, you might decide it's not relevant. So do consider the audience the author is aiming to reach and whether the book is for you.

Of course, I don't have all these questions answered just through quickly flicking through a book, but often quite a few are dealt with through a short scan of cover, Introduction, Contents and Index, which is why it's good to know where to look. So if you've never asked these questions before reading, find a book that looks interesting and start digging. You don't have to have everything answered before deciding to purchase or read a book, but asking searching questions can help, as occasionally I've purchased a book on a whim and regretted it, mainly because I wasn't sufficiently inquisitive.

As I'm reading, some of these questions may well still be in the back of my mind. As I read on, most get answered, especially as I find myself not only engaging with the content but starting to get to know the author. That can be interesting. I feel like I begin to understand who the book-writer is, and how they think. And to some extent that's true, because anyone who writes is doing something really rather revealing, exposing things that they think are important, noteworthy and worthy of consideration. Every author knows this. They discover there's a strange vulnerability to writing. As an author myself I know something of this, understanding that unless a writer bravely rises above any fear of criticism their words will never be published. Authors become a target for people's questions, comments and challenge, even their ridicule and rejection. Some people assume you're trying to make a name for yourself, or trying to get rich, which of course can be true of some writers. In order to check my motives as a writer, I've found the advice of Alister McGrath to be helpful, who found inspiration in C.S. Lewis, 'that a writer is not a spectacle, who says, "Look at me!" Rather, a writer is more like a pair of spectacles, that say "Look through me".'[19] I like that. It has helped give me confidence as a writer and kept me curious as a reader.

Being inquisitive in this way is a developed skill. It aids critical thinking and is a perspective that those seeking wisdom would do well to bring not only to reading books but also to online website content, blogs, as well as news and media channels. Many don't do this. They assume if it's broadcast or printed it must be accurate. The wise know this is not always so.

Discernment

Followers of Jesus, that is, those who are reorientating their lives around the person of Jesus Christ, read to grow wiser, as we will see in more detail in Chapter 4. While they should be willing and open to read all sorts of books and material, the key text for a Christian is the Bible. It always is and always will be, for the Bible is God's inspired message to humanity. It is the book of God, the Word of God, inspired by God. Abraham Lincoln described it as 'the best book that God has given to man',[20] which is why we should prayerfully read it more than any other, and ideally do so daily. The Bible shapes Christian doctrine and belief, as well as our way of life. It has done so for 2,000 years and will continue to do so until the end of time. When it comes to the Bible's interpretation, a simple but helpful axiom is this: when the Bible is clear we can be clear, when the

Bible offers a number of perspectives, we should recognise a number of perspectives.

When it comes to understanding the Bible's message, most people discover it to be refreshingly clear and helpful, with generations of people across a breadth of cultures having found the Bible providing them with helpful instruction, encouragement and guidance for life. Nevertheless, it helps to know that the Scriptures, which were mainly written in Hebrew and Greek, require translation. And it's advantageous to know what kind of literature is before us (e.g. is it narrative, history, poetry, letter, allegory or wisdom literature?). Also the words need to be not only understood, but interpreted and applied, which is especially important with difficult phrases or sections that have been variously understood. This makes the Bible a book to wrestle with. A book to explore. A book to enjoy. And I am never bored, for there's always more to discover in this text of texts. It's why, when I was consecrated as a bishop, which is both the highest – and the lowliest – office in the church, the first thing that happened in the ordination service was that I was handed a Bible, and told: 'Receive this book, as a sign of the authority given you this day to build up Christ's Church in truth. Here are words of eternal life. Take them for your guide and declare them to the world.'[21] The Bible is the most important gift given at any bishop's consecration, with rubrics in the Ordinal (the Service of Ordination) stating: 'It is important that the Giving of the Bible is clearly distinguished from any subordinate ceremonies.'[22]

For bishops, and indeed for all Christians, the Bible is our core text. Not only does it reveal who God is in the person of Jesus Christ, it also gives us hope to help those in need and build a better world. Whether someone believes the Bible is God's authoritative word or not, it *is* a transformative text. It really *has* changed millions of lives, and deeply impacted the cultural history of many nations, and still does. Unsurprisingly, the Bible was written and compiled for that purpose: to cause people to repent which, to put simply, means turn around.[23] The Bible demands our attention. It's not just meant to be a nice read; it's written to be an unsettling read. It's not just meant to make us good; it's written to make the world good.

When it comes to reading other things, there is a Bible passage to which, over the years, many Christ-followers have turned for guidance. It's a passage encouraging Christians in the Roman town of Philippi to be discerning about the kind of things they contemplate. It could apply these days to what we watch on our screens, the kind of conversations we partake in, as well as the words we read. Here's the advice:

> whatever is true, whatever is noble, whatever is right, whatever is pure, whatever is lovely, whatever is admirable – if anything is excellent or praiseworthy – think about such things.
>
> *Philippians 4:8*

These carefully crafted words are a call to take care about the things we let enter our minds, and it is wise advice. As we'll see elsewhere in this book, it doesn't mean we should never read things that are difficult or challenging or painful, but it probably does mean we should avoid things we know to be deliberately damaging and destructive, and needlessly nasty and noxious. This is a further reason why I advocate reading with a disposition of hope.

Reading in this way helps us not only in our personal lives but also as we consider new things that emerge in wider culture. As I say in *A–Z of Discipleship*: 'Sola Scriptura ('Scripture Alone') has been the rallying-cry of many past disciples who've wanted to ensure that change in church and society is change for the good.'[24] When it comes to some of the big moral and ethical questions of the day, after listening to God in Scripture, it's good for Christ-followers to also use the rich resources of *reason* (thinking something through), *tradition* (studying the wisdom of the past) and *experience* (seeing what God is doing today) as secondary means of discernment. These four things – this quadrilateral of discernment – means that with Bible in hand, we use our brains, we read well, and we pay attention to what's happening in us and around us.

Reading well in this way is not just about reading contemporary writers. So much has been written in the past, so if we can, it's helpful to consult ancient words and the thoughts and perspectives of saints of old. Indeed, we neglect their texts at our peril. I see this now more than ever, with many of the books I read these days being quite ancient. For example, when researching for my recent book on fasting – *The Art of Fasting* – I spent much time reading the Church Fathers of the first four centuries AD – people like John Chrysostom and Basil the Great. Not all, but many of the issues we wrestle with today have already been considered in the past by great minds. We would do well to sit down and read them, so we might listen and learn.

Pleasure

There's one more very practical thing I often do to help me create time and space to read, and I know many others do this too. I usually make a drink to sip while reading.

Occasionally I grab a bottle of cold water that's been cooling in the fridge, but most of the time it's a hot drink, like tea or coffee, depending on the time of day. A hot drink and a book always seem to go well together, and of course making the drink shows my intention to read for at least as long as it takes to finish the drink. So the drink helps us focus and give time, and I commend the practice. For me, I want the reading experience to be pleasurable. That means, if I can, I'll make a drink I really enjoy, which is usually an Earl Grey tea or a flat white coffee. With drink in hand, and Kerry pencil by my side, I then find a pleasant space to read, and I'm ready.

Having said this, all you *really* need is a book. And if the book is good, then in the end it doesn't matter if you're reading when thirsty and squashed up on a tube train, or locked in a damp prison cell. The most important thing is to have a book in hand and some time to read.

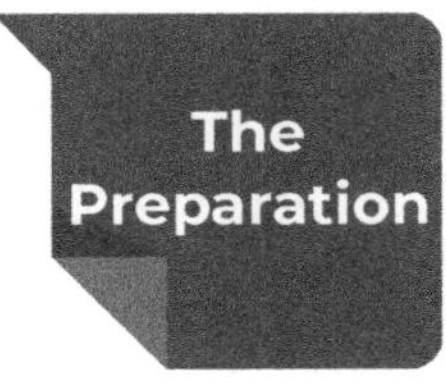

- put your phone to one side

- have a pencil ready to mark up your books

- read attentively, for lifelong learning

- be inquisitive and ask questions – it aids critical thinking

- daily Bible reading helps us read other texts discerningly

- find a good place to read

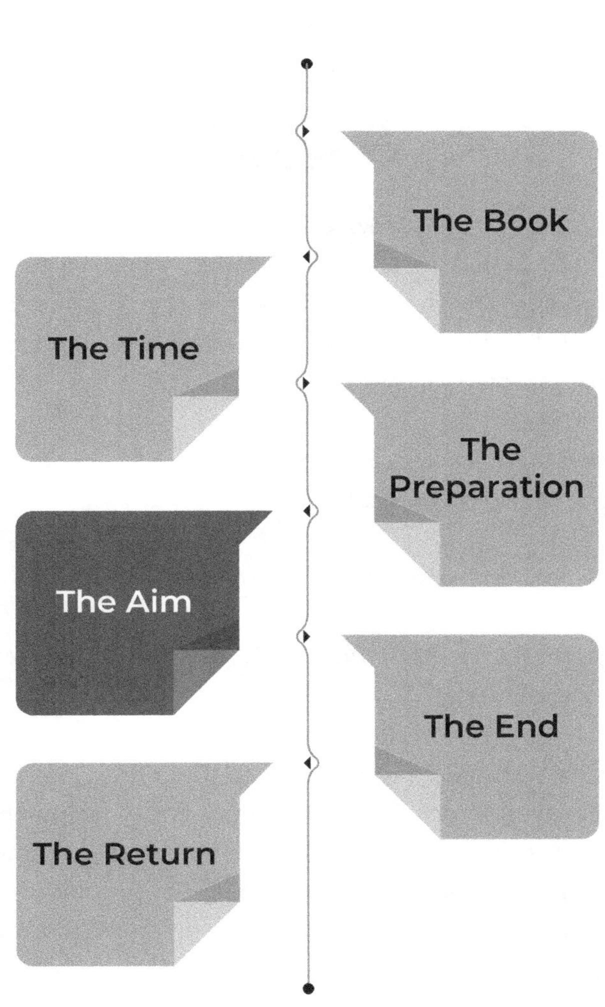

The Book
The Time
The Preparation
The Aim
The End
The Return

Chapter 4

Grow in wisdom

- *'everyone who hears these words of mine and puts them into practice is like a wise man who built his house on the rock' (Matt. 7:24).*

- *'We are drowning in information, while starving for wisdom' (Edward O. Wilson).*[1]

- *'ask good questions' (Hannah Steele).*[2]

- *'Reading is to the mind what exercise is to the body' (Richard Steele).*[3]

There's an aim behind my reading. Rather than just seeking information, I'm pursuing formation.[4] That means I seek to read curiously, carefully and attentively. Whether it's a novel or something more factual, it's important that I read the words, but my intent is much greater. I'm reading to grow. To become more. More the person I'm created to be. More loving. More impactful. If I were to summarise it in a word, it would be that I'm aiming to become *wiser*.

Immersion

I recently read Elizabeth Strout's novel *Tell Me Everything*. I bought it the week it was published and finished it in just a few days. I reflected on it in my journal, surprised at what flowed off my fountain pen, as I wrote: 'I feel like I'm a better person as a result. More connected with people. With pain. With struggle. With frustration. With abuse. With kindness. With love.' I went on to say: 'I've been enlarged by this book.' That's not true of every book I read, and there are no doubt some books which shape us without us consciously realising it, but sometimes I just know a book has touched me at a deep level, capturing my heart and soul. Such a book becomes precious. Acclaimed author William Boyd believes *literature* can do this more than all the other seven arts. While the performing arts of *theatre*, *dance* and *film* are powerful means of communication, and *painting*, *sculpture* and *music* link the artist and consumer often very personally, Boyd believes that 'nothing comes close to the intimacy of writer and reader'.[5] I agree.

Novels are a very powerful form of literary writing. Just go into any High Street bookshop and you'll see that one of, if not the largest section, is *fiction*. That's because people love to read fiction.

Why? Why is fiction so compelling? At a basic level fiction is about story, and we human beings are storytelling creatures. We are made for story, love stories, need stories and enjoy entering into the stories of others.[6] Indeed it's one of the main reasons why I follow Jesus, believing the Christian story truly to be the greatest story ever told. Through stories we find ourselves not just peeking through a keyhole but diving into an ocean – immersing ourselves in vast, rewarding new worlds. Through fiction we learn to like and loathe, to identify and to reject, and when a story captures our attention, we're curious to know what happens next. There is good evidence to show that while many of us read novels simply to be entertained or to escape our own realities, fiction often makes readers more openminded, empathetic and kind.[7] More than we realise, we are formed as we immerse ourselves in stories.

Poetry is a very different form of storytelling genre. It's a particularly powerful kind of literature which I occasionally dip into, recognising it to have the potential to be a deeply immersive reading experience. Poets play with words, constructing a type of writing designed to be compelling and compact, stimulating the imagination and stirring emotion. Poems can often have multiple meanings and be read at a number of levels. They're not best read quickly and even more than fiction, poetry requires the reader to pause and think, reading the words carefully and creatively. This means when I read works by, say, Emily Dickinson or Rupert Brook or Rachel Mann,[8] I know I need to concentrate and focus. If I don't and fail to be aware and alert, I will encounter little of the richness of poetry's fine literary form.

Sometimes I read poems or stories but don't really pay attention. Most of us have had that experience of reading words, but afterwards realising that we've not taken in what we've read. It's the same when we hear audible sounds, with experts often drawing a distinction between hearing and listening. Hearing is the physiological process of attending to the sound, whereas listening is the focused, concentrated approach to understanding what's being heard. We often see this in our human relationships. My wife, for example, knows that when I'm watching football on TV, I can physically hear her speak but I find it really hard to listen! If we apply this to reading, then good reading is not *just* reading words from a page. It's also about avoiding interruptions and unhelpful distractions (see Chapter 3) and really listening to the book. It's about taking care about the content. And it's about being emotionally intelligent and observing the stirrings in my heart and mind and body as I read. It's about being receptive to the story, the ideas, the argument or whatever is being communicated. This is listening immersively, to be changed.[9]

Pace

As I seek to read formationally in this way, at what pace should I read? I'm sometimes asked this – about whether it's best to read fast or slow. My usual answer is that it depends. Some people are just slow readers, although for most of us, the more we read the quicker we become. But in the end the speed depends on the kind of book you're reading and what you are wanting to get from it. There are some books that unless you read every word with care you won't understand it. This is often the case for a novel. But there are other books where we can skip along and read at pace and get the sense of what's happening, even if we miss the odd detail here and there. So it depends on the book and also what you're trying to achieve from the reading.

When I was doing my Masters' degree dissertation on the twentieth-century church leader and evangelist David Watson, I read all his books.[10] It was important that I understood the person and what he was saying, so I read his works carefully and *slowly*. However, when each week I read the Saturday newspaper, I read differently, and mostly I read *quickly*. I skim-read many stories and articles. I will read headlines and opening sections. My eye might jump across various paragraphs, perhaps settling on some key words or particular comments, especially aware of the first and final words at the end of the piece. There's nothing wrong with this. It's speedreading at its best. But then I might come across an article in the paper that fascinates me. I will slow down and read it with precision, wanting to take in what I'm reading.

Skim-reading can work particularly well when studying or reading *non-fiction*. It's not a habit for children to pick up too early, as we all need to learn to read and take in the meaning of a text. But once we're reasonably confident at this, skim-reading is a useful skill to employ and is a good time-saving habit. In fact as I write this, just yesterday I skim-read a 300-page non-fiction book in about an hour and a half; to read it in full might have taken ten hours or more, which is time I didn't have. So instead I opened every page, looking out not only for headings, but observing how each paragraph started and finished, being attentive to key words and phrases. Having a pencil with me was so helpful, as I underlined sections and scribbled in the margins. No doubt I missed some things, but I got the main gist and was able to pull out some useful quotes. This kind of reading can be very helpful and in some jobs which involve much reading, it's the main way people read. For me, it's not a relaxing way to read and afterwards I'm often brain-tired and probably a touch more anxious. This is why it's not my preferred way of reading, although others may differ.

If you really do want to take in what you're reading, you must slow down. It will help you to engage with the text, enabling you to think and reflect and grow. That's why theologian and author Paula Gooder admits: 'One of the things that I have found over the years is that if I can read more slowly and reflectively, I can learn so much more about God, about the world and about myself as I read.'[11] Some people read quickly for their jobs. You may be a teacher, a journalist, a lawyer, or maybe engaged in a course of study, and so you read a lot, and you're encouraged to skim-read. If that's you, take care that you don't translate this into all your reading outside of your work or study programme. Make sure some, indeed much, of your reading is slow, especially when it comes to books. Book reading is not usually a quick process. I've found that sometimes I'll be reading a section of a book which I really want to take in, but I've been skim-reading, forgetting to slow down. The result is that when I get to the end, I notice that I've only got the big picture and not the details, and I then have to go back and read it all again.

So vary the pace; learn to read quickly, and slowly. Particularly slowly.

Wise

Readers who attend to the text and their pace are normally people committed to lifelong learning. They're wanting to develop and change for the good. As we saw in Chapter 1, while this is partly about gaining information, it is much more about transformation. Good reading should form character, changing us and maturing us, making us more human, more generous, more kind, more wise. This is the aim. Wisdom.

Wisdom is at the heart of good reading as reading broadens your knowledge base, exposes you to diverse perspectives and encourages critical thinking – all crucial components of wisdom. I think it should be the main reason for reading. I understand that we sometimes read to escape and be entertained. Or to be inspired and intrigued. Or to research or revisit. Or to discover or delight. But in all these areas and more, what's central is our desire for wisdom. Even somewhat frivolous reading, I would argue, is for this. It's to strengthen, build, equip and motivate, so we can be the best versions of ourselves and fulfil our God-given potential. So we can be wiser.

The Bible has much to say on growing in wisdom. Indeed there is a whole section of literature in the Bible which is known as *Wisdom Literature*, comprising Proverbs, Ecclesiastes, Job, Song of Songs and the Psalms.[12] Proverbs, in particular, was written for the express purpose of helping readers 'know wisdom' (Prov. 1:2, ESV). It seems that God is interested in us becoming wiser people.

Here are five summary things that Scripture as a whole says about wisdom, which influence reading, especially for a follower of Jesus.

First, God the Trinity is the source of wisdom. Romans 16:27 describes God the Father as 'the only wise God'. According to Isaiah 11:2 the Holy Spirit is 'the Spirit of wisdom'. And Jesus is 'wisdom from God' (1 Cor. 1:30), coming as God in human flesh and embodying wisdom. We are invited to live close to Christ, empowered by his Spirit in a respectful relationship with God. This helps us gain his wisdom; this is why Proverbs tells us that reverence for God 'is the beginning of wisdom' (Prov. 1:7, DRA). Augustine of Hippo, the fourth-century African theologian who shaped so much of Christian theology believed this, reflecting on the necessity of faith to achieve wisdom, and that this rested on reading the Scriptures.[13] This has been my experience, finding that reading the Bible enables me to come to know this God more, understanding not only his nature but also his ways (Ps. 103:7).[14]

Second, we can ask God for wisdom. We can pray for wise decision-making and to be people who grow in wisdom. I have been asking for this for much of my life, as Solomon did,[15] doing what it says in James 1:5: 'If any of you lacks wisdom, you should ask God, who gives generously to all without finding fault, and it will be given to you.' I read as part of my answer to that prayer.

Third, we can learn wisdom from others, as we spend time with sages, especially the elderly, who have much life experience. Job 12:12 tells us that wisdom is often found in 'the aged' and that as we value our days and seek to learn well from others, so we can 'gain a heart of wisdom' (Ps. 90:12). Reading is a formational discipline, helping us learn from the wisdom of others.

Fourth, wisdom is expressed not just in words but in action. Indeed 'Of making many books there is no end, and much study wearies the body' (Eccl. 12:12). This means we don't read just to gain wise minds but to live wise lives. Wisdom must be expressed in lifestyle. Jesus could not have been clearer about this, comparing those who hear his words and do *not* put them into practice to fools who build houses on sand, whereas those who hear and *put his words into practice* are like wise people who build on rock. When the storms of life come, it is the wise who stand.[16] Reading, then, must lead to action. It must propel me from my armchair to the street.

Fifth, wisdom is to be shared. Proverbs 4:11 describes being instructed by others 'in the way of wisdom'. This means we are to pass on what we know and help others, who can help others. We don't just read to improve ourselves, but to improve the world. Even people in poverty can read not only to escape their present circumstances but also to assist others: their family, the neighbours and even their community. One of the most influential writers of the

Victorian era, Charles Dickens, is a case in point. Born in 1812, Dickens was the second of eight children and brought up for a time in the poor London neighbourhood of Camden Town. His father went to prison for being in debt in 1824, so Charles had to leave school and work long hours at a shoe-polishing factory, earning six shillings per week. This experience shaped him and his writing, motivating him to write from the perspective of people in material poverty. At the other end of the economic scale, people with wealth can purchase books and open their bookshelves to others, not to show off their vast library, but to share learning and empower readers. This is what artist Pedro Reyes and fashion designer Carla Fernández have done recently with their home *Casa de Carla* in Mexico City, which is a continually adapting architectural project and includes 25,000+ volumes of books, doubling up as a public lending library. Not only does *Casa de Carla* open up a rich resource of creative books to people who would otherwise never have access to such literature, it also encourages those who are less affluent to change and dream new possibilities not just for themselves, but for their families and communities. This kind of formational reading is all about learning to give, share and help others. It's reading grounded in hope and seeking wisdom.

Reading, then, is a helpful discipline for all, especially followers of Jesus. It helps us become wiser people. This is more than accumulating knowledge; it is about living well. Knowledge is the accumulation of facts, information and skills, while wisdom is the ability to apply these things strategically, impactfully and kindly. It seems, then, that Jesus was right: wisdom really is about putting into practice what we read.

Contemplative

There is a form of reading which is particularly helpful for those who read to become wise. It's often overlooked but of great value. It is contemplative reading.

In some circles this kind of reading is called *meditative reading* or even *meditation*, but I tend to call it *contemplative reading* because these days most people consider meditation to be the practice that's come from Eastern philosophical and Buddhist religious traditions, where you empty your mind and wait for enlightenment. That is the opposite of what I want to advocate here, as rather than emptying your mind, contemplative reading is about *filling* it. I've learned this helpful reading technique mainly from the wisdom of various ancient Christian saints, who encourage an immersive reading of the Bible. This practice emerged from the Hebrew notion of meditative reflection, which they discovered by observing the chewing of food by cows – what we often call *rumination*. Cows chew the cud and then swallow it, and then regurgitate it to chew it again, doing this several times, in order to extract all the goodness out of the food. This is the idea behind contemplative reading. It's a means of literary rumination. While it works excellently for reading the Bible, contemplative reading can also work well for many other texts too. Francis Bacon, the English Renaissance philosopher and statesman knew something of this, when he wrote: 'Some books are to be tasted, others are to be swallowed, and some few to be chewed and digested.'[17] This means that sections of books, and even whole books, can be read and read and read, in order to get all you can from them.[18]

Below I share five ways that I sometimes do this. All these examples are helpful when it comes to reading the Bible, so if you've never used any of these tools in Bible reading, have a go. Many down the centuries have used them and found them a wonderful way not only of engaging with holy texts but also of hearing God speak pertinently through them. And yet, these techniques can be used in other forms of literature too. So if you've *only* used them when reading Scripture, apply them more widely. I expect you'll be surprised how useful they are. So, here are the five models:

1. *Lectio Divina*
2. *Character analysis*
3. *Word analysis*

4. *Discovery method*

5. *Journalists' questions*

1. Lectio Divina

Sometimes I will read a story and something stops me short. It could be a twist in the plot, but it might be a turn of phrase or simply one word that triggers a thought or emotion. Rather than racing on to the next section, I will go back and read the section in which it appears a second time. Having done this, I will then re-read it a third time, reflecting why this has caught my attention. It's a very simple thing to do and can be remarkably helpful. In the church this is often called *Lectio Divina* and is an approach to reading the Bible particularly developed by the sixteenth-century Spanish priest Ignatius of Loyola.[19] St Ignatius encouraged this to be done in community, and today it's often done around a table with friends so together we can gain from each other's insights and perspectives. After the first reading each person is normally asked to share a word or phrase from the text that stands out, and then after the second reading to say why, before the final third reading. While this way of reading will slow down my progress through a novel, or work of history, I've found it can be surprisingly helpful, even when I'm on my own, especially when my heart is stirred by a phrase or expression that I've read. It doesn't work for every kind of text, and you will need to ensure the section of words you're reflecting on isn't too long. But it can work well for a breadth of texts, helping us think deeply. If I have time, I will write up my reflections in my journal.

2. Character analysis

Another way of reading any book, which I've learned from reading Scripture, is to identify with a character in the story. Often we read a Bible text which is a story involving a number of people. Rather than reading in a very matter-of-fact, objective manner, I instead imagine myself as one of the people in the story. If, for example, it's a narrative of compassionate healing, like the story of Jesus healing a paralysed man, brought into a crowded house on a stretcher by his friends who made a hole in the roof to lower him down,[20] I might think of myself as the man on the stretcher. I will ask myself questions, like: what is life like for him? How does it feel to be so dependent on others? Is he scared being taken on the roof and then lowered down? What is it like, when the crowd parts, seeing Jesus, and looking up and into his eyes from the floor of the house? So many questions could be asked. If I have time, I can change characters. I will now read the text again but this time from the perspective of, say, one of the man's friends. Or of someone in the house. Or even of Jesus. When we read an interesting novel, most people instinctively find they identify with at least one character in the story. That's fine. But it's also good to shift allegiance and step into the shoes of others too. As we empathise, so we get more out of the text.

3. Word analysis

At other times I will read a much shorter section – even just a few words or a couple of sentences – and pause simply to let what I've read really sink in.[21] Rather than going through a *Lectio Divina* approach of focusing on just one word or phrase, in this model the text is read a number of times, and on each occasion, I focus on a different word. Often the best way to do this is to read the phrase out loud and emphasise a different word each time. So, for example, you might be reading J.R.R. Tolkein's *The Fellowship of the Ring*, and read: 'All we have to decide is what to do with the time that is given us.'[22] You could read it a number of times, the first time accentuating the word 'All' and then the second time 'decide' and the third 'do' etc. Again, this can be a surprisingly powerful and moving technique, if we're willing to ponder on the things that come to mind as we contemplate.

4. Discovery method

Occasionally when I read, I ask particular questions which encourage a personal response to what's been read. The *Discovery Bible Study* method, which is now used all over the world, does this simply and well, asking of a Bible passage: a) What do I learn about God? b) What do I learn about people? c) How should I respond? d) Who else needs to hear this? These are four great questions of any text, to which I might also ask: What am I grateful for in the text? What emotions has this stirred in me? What have I learned about the world? Is there something I should start doing, or stop doing? These kinds of questions can be asked at the end of a short section of any text that has moved me, at the close of a chapter that's made me think, or even when I've finished a book – as we will see later.

5. Journalists' questions

Sometimes I will use the *Journalists' questions* when reading a text, asking: *Who? What? Where? When? How?* and *Why?* These questions work well for short Bible passages but they can also work for any story, of any length. Here's how. *Who?* Most stories involve people. Characterisation is central. It's what makes stories interesting. *What?* Something happens. It could be very ordinary or extraordinary. Certainly something noteworthy. *Where?* People and events are always rooted in places and spaces. The environment and setting are not unimportant. *When?* Stories always happen in time. Maybe last year, or 1,000 years ago. *How?* How did the event happen? And how did the people respond and the plot unfold? *Why?* Purpose is sometimes explained but not always. Sometimes the reason for, or behind, the story emerges or needs discerning, or is left to the reader. The question of *Why?* is often the intriguing question left hanging for the reader, propelling them to read more. While I've occasionally structured a talk or preach based around these journalists' questions, I normally ask them simply for myself as part of my preparation, to help me understand. The questions can create a helpful framework, enabling me to see what's happening. Like any technique, it has its limits and if overused can create a hyper-analytical approach to a text that sometimes just needs reading and enjoying. That's why it's just one of several models which encourage good and deep thinking. Interestingly, this kind of attentive, observant, character-forming reading is why the apostle Peter wrote his letters and wanted them read.[23]

There are many other ways to read contemplatively, but these five models offer a good starting point and can be applied beyond Scripture. I've learned them mainly through Bible reading, by engaging in what Anglican philosopher and theologian Austin Farrer called 'the forbidding discipline of spiritual reading',[24] and they've helped me in my own discipleship, and in my role as a Bible teacher, but they can be applied more broadly to most texts. If one or more of them is new to you, choose one and have a go. And even try doing it with others, as you read a text out loud and reflect together, as many books – from the Bible to many great pieces of poetry and prose – were intended to be first heard as spoken words.[25]

Collective

Having someone read *to* you and *with* you is a good way to read and listen thoughtfully. As we've seen, this is especially so when reading a sacred text, like the Bible. Years ago, when only the educated could read, this is how most people heard stories and learned. Someone would read to them. That's how, for example, Paul's letters would have been initially received when they were sent to churches, like those in Corinth or Colosse: someone would have stood before them and read it as everyone listened. This means they would have been heard audibly – in the same way we listen to someone reading aloud a story today. In past generations, storytellers were respected and honoured, with storytelling a cherished artform. There were even professional storytellers who would make their living travelling from village to village and telling stories. It was a form of hearing the news. It's good to see, in some sectors of contemporary Western society, the role of storyteller beginning to re-emerge again.

Children enjoy having a book read to them, as we saw in Chapter 2. One of the reasons author S.F. Said writes for children today is that he remembers Mr Evans, his schoolteacher, reading to the class on a Friday afternoon, and how that was the highlight of his school week. Rather than having to take notes, or be tested, instead 'he just read to us' and 'we weren't asked to do anything but listen'.[26] Children often get lost in a story, and it can be a delightful experience to read to a child, not only in the day but also at bedtime. Many of us will have had this experience in our childhood, and if we have children or grandchildren, we've probably done this with them and know how much they enjoy this. But at some point this normally stops. It's usually when children start to become confident about reading for themselves. They want to be grown-up and think being read to is just for little children. But that's not true. While eighteenth-century philosopher Rousseau was right to advocate that children should learn to read on their own,[27] we now know there's great benefit in having someone reading to us as adults. It's not only fun, but it's good for us. In fact, scientific research shows that we use different parts of our brain to read and to listen.[28] So having someone read to us is another means of listening well.

For three and a half years, up until 2020, we had a young man living in our household who originates from East Africa. He had to flee from his country as a teenage political refugee, and he ended up in the UK. He told me how most evenings when he was a child he would sit with his family around a fire and listen to stories. His father especially would tell stories about family members, about wartime and about the oppression of his tribal people.

He loved hearing these stories. It reminded me that this is what human beings have been doing for thousands of years – gathering and telling and listening to stories. There is an art to both – not just to the telling, but to the listening. If we can learn to listen thoughtfully, then the words come alive. We can enjoy the listening and we can grow.

The same is true when someone reads a book to me. It may be a live person, reading a story in the same room as me, or at a book-reading event, or even on stage. Or it could be down the phone or on video, or an audiobook while walking to work or driving in the car. Being read to is *so* good! That's why, when the UK government told everyone in 2020 to stay at home to avoid coronavirus and to protect the NHS, I asked the publishers of one of my books if I could record a daily video reading of it and post it online, and they agreed.[29] It not only attracted some new listeners, but people engaged with the book differently by listening to it being read to them.

For many, reading is a solitary pastime. That's especially true for those living in the individualistic West. But that's not always been the case. Up to the age of Enlightenment in the eighteenth century, reading out loud was not only considered normal, it was also deemed necessary in order to gain a full understanding of a text. For example, St Augustine of Hippo, who lived in the fourth and fifth centuries AD, believed that within the confines of a page the *scripta*, the written words, had to become *verba*, spoken words, in order to spring into being. For Augustine, the reader was powerful. Their role was to breathe life into a text by speaking it out loud, thus filling the created space with living words. This is why the verbal reading of Scripture in public has always been important in acts of Christian worship. As we begin to understand from empirical research the creative power of the spoken word,[30] so we recognise that there may well be some scientific reason behind this ancient practice. That's why it's good to see communal reading out loud making something of a comeback today, for it's a form of reading which, in my opinion, is powerful and highly underrated.

There are many ways we can read a book, including having someone read to us. So be creative. Explore new avenues. Listen thoughtfully. Approach reading with this kind of attitude, and you will find it renewing, refreshing and reviving. And don't just read the words. Let the words read you. As you seek transformation, read hopefully. Enter in. Explore. Ask questions. Seek meaning. Seek enlightenment, and as you do, you will grow in wisdom.

- listen thoughtfully

- recognise your reading pace

- read to gain wisdom

- read the Bible and other texts contemplatively

- read collectively – with others

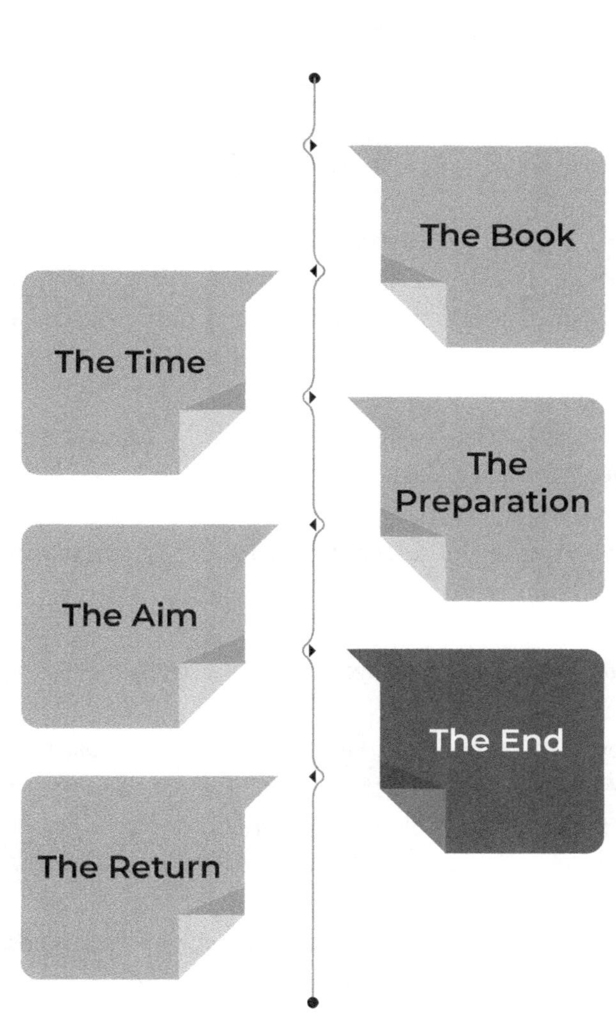

The Book
The Time
The Preparation
The Aim
The End
The Return

Chapter 5

Finish with strength

- *'May my meditation be pleasing to him, as I rejoice in the Lᴏʀᴅ' (Ps. 104:34).*

- *'To read without reflecting is like eating without digesting' (Edmund Burke).*[1]

- *'the mature leader, the best leader, is by nature reflective' (Stephen Cottrell).*[2]

- *'Hurry ruins saints as well as artists' (Thomas Merton).*[3]

When they reach the final word of a book, most people close it and end things there. They're pleased to have finished and so the book is put down, put away or put out. I now do something very different when I finish a book.

I normally place the book to one side for a short period of time to gather my thoughts – perhaps a few minutes or at the most a few days – and then I return to it. I know from experience that coming back to it can be a very difficult thing to do. Maybe it's because of that deeply satisfying sense we get when we've finished a book; we've reached a milestone and achieved something, and it feels right to close it and move on. Also we might have lots of things to do, which we've put off until we finish the book; now the book is read we might feel compelled to get on with those things. But over time I've learned *not* to put the book away and rush on. Why? Because there's further life to receive, flavour to savour and wisdom to gain. Instead I push myself to go past that sense of having finished, because I know I haven't. Not quite. There's still more to do if I'm really going to get the most out of the book.

So here's what I've now learned to do. I catch my breath, return to it again, and do four things.

1. Re-reading

First, I go through the book, page by page and look again at my pencil markings. I take note of everything I've under-lined, circled and scribbled. It only takes a few minutes to do this, and believe me, it is *so* helpful. Having completed the book, re-reading my comments and markings enables me to see the book as a whole and to reflect both on the detail as well as the big picture. Also I'm sure I remember more about it later by doing this.

2. *Quoting*

Second, I do something which I call 'pull out the quotes'. What this means is that I go back through my scribblings and I record any useful quotations, illustrations or ideas, for future use. As a speaker and writer, this provides an invaluable resource for me. It's great to be able to quote Brené Brown as I'm talking about leaving behind shame,[4] or Sir Alex Ferguson when I'm advising about building a team for the long-haul.[5] Gathering information from a finished book in this way can take anything from five minutes to over an hour. However long it takes, this is *always* worth doing. Always.

Years ago I used to record the quotations on index cards, but then my son Ben helped computerise everything for me using *Evernote* software, which has proved really helpful.[6] Even though I will need to choose a heading under which to file things, computerisation means I can come back later and cross-reference through a key word, including authors, which enables me to easily find in the future most of what I want to retrieve in just a few seconds. Gathering the quotes doesn't need to be done by computer, so if you're not computer literate, or can't afford a computer, a card index would suffice, but if you can computerise using some simple software, there are many benefits. This *Quotes* resource is now one of my most valuable possessions, being the fruit of years and years of reading and recording.

3. Journalling

Third, I normally write about the book in my journal. I keep a regular journal which I write in every few days. It's not a diary where I record what I've done, rather it's my reflections on life. It's personal, just for me. All sorts of things go in there – from comments about family, friends, church, politics and the weather, to thanksgivings, regrets, moans, hopes, prayers, dreams, insights and more. I highly recommend journalling as a key habit of effective people and disciplined disciples. Indeed, the second book in this *Art of . . .* series, is all about journalling.[7] So when I've finished a book, I normally comment on it in my journal. This gives me further time to meditate on and consider what I've been discovering through reading this book. There may be a theme which has stirred something in me and maybe the odd choice quotation that I've now captured and is filed for future use. Perhaps there's some factual information that has lodged in my mind, or a comment that's deeply stirred my heart. I often take stock of the message of the whole book, describing what I've discovered and how it has impacted me. Most importantly, there may be an action I need to pursue. As I read to be formed and grow in wisdom – and wisdom is always reflected in action – this is the main reason for returning to the book: it helps me respond. To do this well, I pray. I will cover all this reflective journalling in prayer, asking the Lord to help me, guide me, lead me, change me, empower me and use me.

Good journalling should be a prayerful process, and journalling my reading is one of the most lovely and lifegiving things I do.

4. *Listing*

Fourthly and finally, I record the book in my *List of Books*. This is a lined hardback notebook that I've had for a few years in which I record every whole book that I read. Despite knowing I've missed recording quite a few, and recognising that I don't record partly read books, this incomplete record of my reading nevertheless has its benefits. Each new book is numbered after the one before, and I write the author, title and copyright details. I also add when I started, when I finished it, and who owns it. Here's an example:

No.	Author & Name & Details	Started	Finished	Owner
440	Makoto Fujimura, *Art + Faith* (New Haven: Yale Uni Press, 2020).	May 2021	June 2021	MP

I do this for a variety of reasons. Sometimes I remember reading a book on a certain subject say, three years ago, but I can't remember the details. So I go to this *List of Books* and can normally identify it quickly. It also helps me see how many whole books I've read in the past year. I aim for at least one per month, sometimes managing much more than that. If I haven't read at least twelve whole books in a year I conclude that I've been too busy and need to make some adjustments. Finally, I can use my *List of Books* to look back over a period of time and see the *kind* of books I've been reading, enabling me to consider whether my reading diet is remaining good and healthy.

Sharing

Having done these four final things, all of which help me capture the learning, I then seek to share the learning. That can happen in all sorts of ways. It might be as simple as talking about the book, in conversations with people or perhaps in a work context or even over supper. Some people are part of book clubs, where a book is read with others and then the group meet to talk about it. While I've never been part of a book club to date, I hope I will one day, knowing a number of people who find it so helpful. I know that book clubs are also excellent ways of crossing social divides, as people from a range of backgrounds and perspectives can meet to chat about a book.

Keeping

Having squeezed all the goodness out of a book, if it's mine – and it often is – I then put the book away on a book-shelf in my library. I try to put it with similar books so I can easily locate it again. If it's excellent, I'll occasionally buy a copy for someone who I think will value it, especially if they live on a tight budget. Because I'm an author, it's fairly likely that I'll return to the book again at some point for writing purposes, so I normally keep my books. I occasionally lend but normally don't give away my copy. And I certainly don't like to throw books away but believe it's worth developing a library, not just for myself but also for the next generation. South African writer, activist and political analyst Sisonke Msimang agrees, saying she retains her books, wanting her children's children and those yet to be born to be able to read them 'to learn how to pass time, to stave off boredom, to learn new words'.[8]

There are varying views on whether books should be kept. There's a trend today to tidy up and keep our homes minimalistic. I actually quite like that and value decluttering – apart from when it comes to books. I find the advice of Marie Kondo, author of *The Life-Changing Magic of Tidying Up*, helpful when she says:

> Books that have stayed too long on the shelf have become part of the scenery. Only by taking each one in your hands can you actually see them as separate entities. Ask yourself when did you buy it? How many times have you read it? Do you want to read it again? And whether you would still buy that book if you saw it in a bookstore.

Kondo goes on to say that 'sometimes people ask me how many books they should keep, but there's no fixed number. If books spark joy for you, then the correct choice is to keep as many as you want with confidence'.[9]

So have a plan about what you'll do when you get to the end of a book. Pause and take a breath, and don't fail to record and reflect on your learning, thinking you're too busy. 'Busy is the new lazy' says Robert Poynton, author of *Pause*. 'Busy keeps things the same; hectic, but unchanging. It is a kind of avoidance, and that's lazy,' he says.[10] He's right, and so apply this to reading. Go back over a book before moving on, and find a way to be able to locate it when you need it again. That's how you finish well.

- don't put a book away as soon as it's finished

- re-read your scribbles

- 'pull out the quotes'

- reflect on your reading in your journal

- keep a record of what you've read

- find a way to easily access the book again

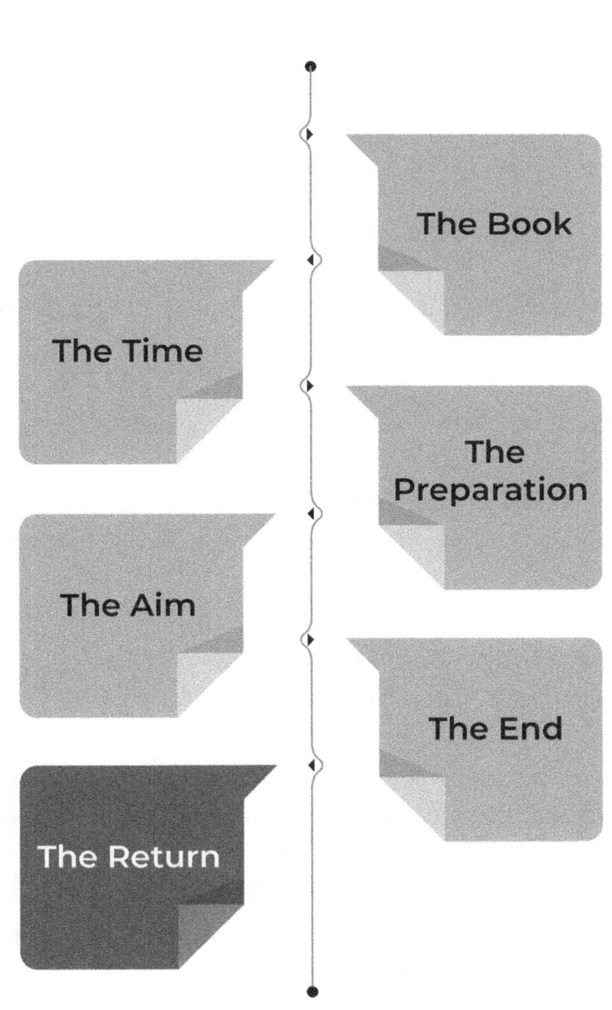

The Book
The Time
The Preparation
The Aim
The End
The Return

Chapter 6

Re-read with regularity

- *'endurance produces character, and character produces hope' (Rom. 5:4, ESV).*

- *'It is a good rule, after reading a new book, never to allow yourself another new one till you have read an old one in between. If that is too much for you, you should at least read one old one to every three new ones' (C.S. Lewis).*[1]

- *'Keep reading. It's one of the most marvellous adventures that anyone can have' (Lloyd Alexander).*[2]

- *'To read is to empower. To empower is to write. To write is to influence. To influence is to change. To change is to live' (South African author, anonymous).*[3]

When I've finished and finally put away a book, here's what I do. I start reading another.

I'd recommend that you don't wait until you end a book before you consider what's next. As you can see the book coming to an end, or maybe even well before, give thoughtful consideration to what you will read after that one. I often have a few ready and lined up to read, so I can get going straight away.

Diet

You might want to consider what *kind* of book you will read next. As I've mentioned already in this small book, I recommend having a good and broad diet of reading. Don't always restrict yourself to your usual circle of books. Try something new. Maybe ask a friend or colleague what they're reading and check it out. Stretch yourself. So after having read a lightweight novel, I may decide to read something different, like a book on popular music, or a text on the developing science of sleep research. Or I might choose to read three novels in a row by the same author, especially if the one I've finished is the first part of a trilogy, or maybe I just like how they write and want more.

Marie Kondo, mentioned in the previous chapter, advises that it's important to consider whether you will read the book again. I agree. Some people question whether you should ever read a book again. The answer is *yes*, and I'm increasingly doing this. It's like returning to a good film and observing things I didn't notice the first time. The reason for this, according to Alberto Manguel, is that 'A book becomes a different book every time we read it',[4] so he can confidently declare, 'You never dip into the same book twice'[5] for we are different people when we pick up a book again. We have changed. So read again. And enjoy the experience. Argentine author Jorges Luis Borges loved to do this, famously saying, 'I prefer rereading to reading'.[6] C.S. Lewis similarly wrote: 'Clearly one must read every good book at least once every ten years',[7] being keen to return to fine literature, allowing its words to lodge deep in his heart and mind.

Most fields have widely respected works that it's good to read and re-read. Be it Sun Tzu, Peter Drucker and Cheryl Sandberg on leadership; William Shakespeare, Charlotte Brontë and Charles Dickens in English literature; Gerald Manley Hopkins, Sylvia Plath and Maya Angelou in poetry; or Aristotle, Angela Duckworth and Susan Caine on developing resilient character, it's good to regularly rediscover the richness of great writing. Authors like these and their words are wise and wonderful, offering good gifts for inquisitive readers.

Displaying
Returning to a book requires you to be able to find it again. If you don't own it you could locate it in your local library, but if it's already yours and on your bookshelf, you can just

pull it out again, assuming you arrange your books in such a way that you can easily find it. This is why I recommend sorting your books for easy access into categories, including genre, theme and author, as you create your own library at home. This library will increasingly express something of your taste and priorities, reflecting themes, ideas and authors that you think are important. That's partly what gatherings of books do, which is why I love exploring people's libraries. Not only do I find interesting things that I might read, but I learn much about the person behind the library.

Not everyone has the space for a whole room to be a library, but part of a room, or perhaps a hallway or landing can become library-like. Even if you don't have many books or are on a low income and can't afford very much, you can still display what you have in some form or another, even if it's only on one shelf. Don't do this to show off. The purpose is not to demonstrate how wise you are, but to ensure your books are accessible because they're cherished and of educational and developmental value. Some people get worried about the kind of statement this makes to anyone who comes into your house. If you're concerned about that, I recommend that you recognise that everything in your home says something: not just the layout of rooms but the pictures on your wall, and the things you display or don't. There's nothing wrong with having books around and available. You're telling yourself and all who enter your house that reading is important. Because it is.

Sharing

Often when I've read a good book that's helped me in some way or another, and I talk to others about it, or mention it in a blog or in conversation with someone, I'm then asked if I would lend the book. Sometimes I do, although I've found by experience that the majority of books I lend don't come back. So these days when I'm asked if I'll lend a book, I'm more careful before I hand it over. If I know I'll need the book in the next few weeks for something (e.g. referencing it in a talk or in my writing) or if I've scribbled something of a personal nature in it, I will politely decline, perhaps guiding the person requesting to a secondhand copy online. Otherwise I say *yes*, but before I lend it, I do two things.

First, I make sure I've written the details of the book, and who I'm lending it to, in my *Lending Notebook*. That way I know, rather like a library, which books are 'out' and I can track them down in the future, if necessary. If I forget to do this, which I sometimes do, I probably won't remember later who I've lent it to.

Second, I check my name is in the front of the book. These days when I start a book, I write in the inside cover my name and the date and place where I begin reading it. In recent years I've started to mark that page with a little embossed stamp that my wife gave me, which says 'Library of Matthew Porter'. Doing these things are not only helpful to me but also mean that if the book disappears from my library, it's just a little more likely to get returned.

In the end, a book that doesn't come back can normally be replaced. So if it doesn't return but has helped someone else, that's good. But to be totally honest, being a book lover *and* someone who wants to be generous is a combination which often leaves me in a dilemma when I'm asked to lend a book. Shall I lend it, or not? It helps to keep reminding myself that books are gifts – and gifts are to be shared.

Leadership

When I read and re-read, I also need to keep remembering *why* I'm reading. It's for wisdom. It's to be an effective disciple of Jesus. It's so I grow and change and become a more mature, better-equipped human being who makes a difference in the world. Many writers see this, with Alberto Manguel seeing reading as 'the ability to enter a text and explore it to one's fullest individual capacities'.[8]

Down the centuries many political regimes have understood this, with oppressive governments even today seeking to control what people read and destroy that which they deem subversive. Reading can be a dangerous exercise. Readers who grasp this recognise that their reading can be powerful and revolutionary – not just for them, but for those who will be influenced as they faithfully pass on their wisdom. That's why leaders must be readers. Veteran leader and commentator Henry Kissinger agrees, describing in his book entitled *Leadership* how reading helps leaders gain a sense of proportion, and when linked with reflection and the training of the memory, offers a storehouse of knowledge from which leaders can learn. Kissinger goes on to describe how reading well provides perspective and inspiration, recognising that books record the action of leaders 'who once dared greatly, as well as those who dared too much, as a warning'.[9] Reading, then, is crucial for those seeking to influence others. We need to be resourced. And we need to be sure that our ideas and plans are well rooted. Reading helps this like no other discipline. That's why I urge leaders to read carefully and courageously, widely and winsomely, prayerfully and prophetically.

Wiser

In the end, I read to become wiser. In the biblical tradition, wisdom is not just *knowing* the truth, it's *living* it. I want to understand God, his world and humanity and find my place, making a positive difference. I want to do all I can to help people see the wonder of Christ and find fresh identity and loving forgiveness in him, and as a result live lives of kindness and hope, impacting others for good. I want my reading to help me to live this way. Indeed, I want my reading to first change *me* – my mind, my heart and my actions. John Wesley, the founder of the missional Wesleyan movement agreed, saying that people who grow in grace should correspondingly 'grow themselves in reading'.[10] I've found that regular reflective journalling really helps with this, as does talking about books with others. But given that life is short I must go beyond reflecting and talking and turn my reading into action, in my family, church, community and beyond. This is about influencing others and making an impact. That's why Damon Young is right when he says, 'Reading is an introduction to a more ambitious life.'[11] Good reading must do this. Good reading should overflow in good living.

Reading strategically in this way should result in us building a better world. If more people read, and did so intentionally and prayerfully, seeking wisdom, it should help see poverty diminish, hope flourish, fear decrease, cruelty lessen, kindness increase and love grow. As a follower of Jesus and bishop in the church, I want people to come to know the grace of God, found in Jesus Christ, the One who gave up his life that we might have life, now and into eternity. And I want to see villages and towns being served by strong, vibrant local churches full of new and old believers, led by visionary servant leaders, growing churches that are resourcing their communities. In the end, only God can do this, but history shows us he tends to do this through ordinary people, who are humble and prayerful, and curious and compassionate. Good reading helps us become such people.

Reading should enable us to become – to use the present language of the Church of England – 'missionary disciples' in God's wonderful world. Scientist, theologian and apologist Alister McGrath agrees, saying, 'There are, of course, some people I would love to have known as mentors. Sadly I shall never be able to know great writers of the past, such as Augustine of Hippo, Athanasius of Alexandria or Martin Luther . . . Yet I can read their books.' McGrath knows that while reading a book is no substitute for having a living teacher, nevertheless reading allows him 'to absorb their ideas and work out how I might benefit from their wisdom. Though dead, they still speak to us, offering us encouragement and stimulus'.[12] Eighteenth-century revivalist and social reformer John Wesley felt the same, being not only an avid reader, but saying to his leaders: 'It cannot be that the people should grow in grace unless they grow themselves in reading. A reading people will always be a knowing people . . . Press this upon them with your might, and you will soon see the fruit of your labours.'[13] For

Wesley, leaders should model and teach their people to be readers. So read.

Read well. Read broadly. Read imaginatively. Read trans-formationally. Read hopefully. And keep learning to read better. In doing so you will become a wiser person, impacting the world for good.

As you pursue *The Art of Reading*, read to change the world.

- have another book ready

- digest a broad and diverse diet of reading

- good books should be regularly re-read

- read prayerfully and prophetically

- enjoy growing in wisdom as you read

- read to change the world

Afterword

Becoming readers

- *'After this letter has been read to you, see that it is also read in the church of the Laodiceans and that you in turn read the letter from Laodicea' (Col. 4:16).*

- *'The whole world opened up to me when I learned to read' (Mary McLeod Bethune).*[1]

- *'If we encounter a man of rare intellect, we should ask him what books he reads' (Ralph Waldo Emerson).*[2]

- *'There are many little ways to enlarge your child's world. Love of books is the best of all' (Jackie Kennedy Onassis).*[3]

One of my favourite things in life has been watching my sons begin to develop a passion for reading. I hope they will look back on their formative years and say, with author Marilynne Robinson, 'When I was a child I read books.'[4]

Now in their twenties and thirties, they all read. I love seeing them curled up in a chair with a book and I smile, wondering what's going on in their minds. They now put books on their Christmas list. They talk about what they're reading. They even recommend books to me that they think I'll enjoy.

I've often thought that if I can instil in my family a love for reading, and encourage them to read well – rather like I've sought to do in this book – then I've done something important, setting them up for life. Of course there are other things I want and pray for my children, but deep down I know that encouraging them to become readers is a foundational skill for all who are curious about life.

When I was a boy, I remember my elderly grandfather liked to do two things – to paint and to read. When I visited my grandparents' home I would go into the kitchen and enjoy some of my granny's home-baking. I'd then go into the sitting room and there would be Grandpa Luther, who would have either a paintbrush in his hand, or a book on his lap. By this stage in his life he was hard of hearing, struggling from severe age-related deafness. I didn't think about it at the time, but I now realise that deafness can be very socially isolating. Voices from the outside are stilled. Feelings of loneliness are common. Aware that deafness from ageing might come to me one day, I sometimes wonder what it would be like to be deaf like Grandpa, and how I would cope. If that happened, I think I might do what Grandpa did: I would try to develop my creative gifts and I would especially *read*. In fact, I suspect I would spend a great deal of time reading books. Not only is it good preparation for the reading that's going to take place in heaven,[5] but it's also a great means of us hearing. Because when we read, we're spoken to. When we read, a multitude of voices converse with us. When we read, we are never alone.

Appendix

Questions & Answers

In this short Appendix I answer ten common questions that people have about reading. They're questions sometimes asked of me. Most of these have, over time, been my questions too. So here's my Q & A:

1. What should I do if I find a book boring?
Unless you must read it as a compulsory part of studying, for work, or for something similar, don't read a boring book. Life is too short. Move on and find something interesting.

2. What about people who don't find reading easy or enjoyable?
If you're a parent and your children don't enjoy reading as they get older, do your best to help them to enjoy stories. So read to them and encourage them to listen to audiobooks. Help them find a magazine or a podcast related to a hobby. Maybe show them short online articles, or even take them to an interesting modern library, like The Word

in South Shields. Try to enable them to find a subject that interests them and do all you can to encourage them to persevere. Quite a lot of people find reading difficult, especially in teenage years, so talk to them about that, and if that was true for you, tell them your story. I liked having stories read to me when I was a child, and I lived in a house where there were quite a lot of books around. Despite this, as a teen, I found reading for myself increasingly difficult; it just didn't come naturally to me, so much so that I'd have said that I didn't enjoy reading. That meant, other than children's stories, I didn't read a whole book until my late teens, and even then it was hard work. But I had an English teacher at school – Roger Freebairn – who was passionate about literature and about reading. The way he described books and his joy of reading began to rub off on me, so I persevered. And by the time I reached my early twenties I found that I looked forward to reading. Looking back, I'm so glad I stuck at it, as books are now such an important part of my life. When we move house, the biggest pile of boxes is the one full of books. So if you find reading difficult, keep going. Find a book that looks interesting, make some space, and begin to read.

3. What if someone gives me a book to read?

I thank them very much, but I never promise to read it. If they insist that you read it, you should be honest and give it back. If it's a book of 500 pages that will take many hours to read, it will be a huge chunk of your precious time. What if it's dull? Or just isn't relevant to your life right now? Even if they have good intentions, be careful of people manipulating you and dictating your use of time in this way.

4. Does that mean I should say *no* to every book that is given me?

No. It's possible that you might be given or receive a book that is timely and just what you need to read at this time, so be open to that. Also, many of us read based on the recommendation of others, so listen when a trusted friend or someone you respect speaks highly of a book.[1] Just take care and don't promise you'll read it.

5. Is it OK to skip chapters or sections of a book?

Yes. There are no rules to say you must read every single word or chapter in a book. C.S. Lewis said, 'It is a very silly idea that in reading a book you must never "skip." All sensible people skip freely when they come to a chapter which they find is going to be no use to them.'[2]

6. What if a book looks interesting but as I read I find it hard to understand?

Find a dictionary or use online tools which help explain key terms. However, one of the marks of a good author is that they're able to make complex things simple. So if a book is constantly hard to understand, I would stop and look for a less complex book on the same subject. There's nothing wrong with a well-written simple guide.

7. Are there things I should avoid reading, especially as a follower of Jesus?

It's good to read widely and important to be open to new ideas. But not all books are good books and some just aren't worth reading, especially books that are dark and glorify horrible things like abuse, sadism, extreme violence and graphic sexual excess. I would particularly advise avoiding the genres of *occult* and *pornography*. As you read, take note of your emotions (e.g. what's this doing for my heart? Is it transforming me, for good?). If you're still not sure, check your motives and aims (e.g. will it help me become wiser?). If the answer is *no* and/or you're reading for purely selfish reasons, put it down. You can also ask others who you trust. I've occasionally stopped reading a book because I knew it just wasn't doing me any good. Two or three times I've thrown a book away, not wishing anyone to read it. To paraphrase Jesus: what goes in tends to be what comes out.[3] So read discerningly, and don't forget we only have one life, so don't spend it reading rubbish.

8. Is reading just for the wealthy? And how can people in poverty enjoy the art of reading?

Books are for everyone, whether you're rich or poor, as long as you can read. But let's be honest, it's easier for people of affluence to buy books than those on low incomes. Nevertheless, it's possible to read a broad diet of books even if money is tight. That's why throughout this book something is said about how those on low incomes can access books and reading resources. The main thing is to be intentional, and to make good use of libraries as well as secondhand bookshops. Reading doesn't have to cost the earth.

9. Does it matter if I only read blogs, articles and substacks, rather than books?

Yes, it does matter. Blogs and online resources are helpful in many ways, and are often good at summarising the thinking of others, but they're not the same as reading a book. Especially core texts. So if you can, don't read the Shakespearean summary, read Shakespeare. Don't read about Barack Obama, read Obama. Don't read the daily devotional summary of the Scripture reading, pick up a Bible and read. Listen to audiobooks, as being read to by others can also be helpful, but most of all, read *books*. Books are for life. Books bring life.

10. Will there be books in the future? Won't they die out, now there's so much digital information online?

Human beings love to communicate and much of this is through writing, which of course involves reading. So we're not going to stop reading. As for books, experts in the book world think it's unlikely that they'll cease being produced. Clearly there's a huge and growing amount of information online, including millions of digital books that can be read on phones, Kindle, eBooks and similar platforms. Nevertheless, as I write this in 2025, more physical books than ever are still being printed. It looks like people's appetite for reading hasn't declined, and there's also a growing amount of evidence showing that many people prefer reading a physical book to an eBook. It seems that most of us like holding an actual book in our hands. We like the feel and the physical experience of reading from a proper book – especially a hardback. It may be, though, that in the future fewer books are produced, especially to save paper and trees. If so, having a library of books will be increasingly rare and something of great value.

Acknowledgements

This book is dedicated to my second son, Joel Porter. I love your creative mind, your adventurous spirit and your kind heart. I know that some of this has come from your reading. Joel, may you enjoy growing deeper in wisdom as you keep practising *The Art of Reading*.

I am grateful to Roger Freebairn, my A level teacher of English Literature, who instilled in me a love of reading, and to all those who regularly ask me what I'm reading, particularly my mother, Christine Porter.

Thank you to those who read initial manuscripts of this book, including Gary Everett, Claire Gough, Paul Harcourt, Ben Porter, Sam Porter and Eve Ridgeway. Your insights and advice are greatly appreciated.

Resources

As well as exploring the Notes to this book, readers who value further resources might find it interesting to read:

Steven Roger Fischer, *A History of Reading* (London: Reaktion Books, 2003, 2019).

Keith Houston, *The Book: A Cover-to-Cover Exploration of the Most Powerful Object of Our Time* (New York: W.W. Norton & Company, 2016).

C.S. Lewis, *The Reading Life* (London: William Collins, 2019).

John Man, *The Gutenberg Revolution* (London: Bantam Books, 2009).

Alberto Manguel, *A Reader on Reading* (New Haven, CT: Yale University Press, 2010).

Karen Swallow Prior, *On Reading Well: Finding the Good Life through Great Books* (Grand Rapids, MI: Brazos Press, 2018).

C. Robledo, *The Insightful Reader: How to Learn Deeply & Attain Life-Changing Insights from Books* (I.C. Robledo's Books, 2020).

Virginia Woolf, *How Should One Read a Book* (Kindle Edition; first published 1926).

Notes

Introduction

[1] This much cited quotation is widely attributed to British author and publisher Helen Exley. See, e.g. M.P. Singh, *Quote Unquote* (New Delhi: Lotus Press, 2007), p.57.

[2] Alberto Manguel, *A Reader on Reading* (New Haven, CT & London: Yale University Press, 2010), p.274. Alberto Manguel is an Argentine-Canadian anthologist, translator, essayist, novelist, editor and a former director of the National Library of Argentina.

[3] Eugene H. Peterson, *Eat This Book* (London: Hodder, 2006), p.177.

[4] Peterson, *Eat This Book*, p.177.

[5] Warren, now in his seventies, is still a great advocate for reading. In a 2014 blog he gives four reasons why reading is essential, which in summary are: 1) You must read for inspiration and motivation; 2) You must read to sharpen your skills; 3) You must read to learn from others; 4) You must read to stay current in a changing world. See Rick Warren, 'To Be a Great Leader you must Absolutely Become a Great Reader', 23 October 2014, https://pastors.com/great-leader-absolutely-must-reader/ (accessed 13 April 2020).

[6] See, e.g. https://www.theguardian.com/education/2023/may/16/reading-ability-of-children-in-england-scores-well-in-global-survey (accessed 28 September 2024).

7   I agree with Virginia Woolf that when reading it is important to 'follow your own instincts, to use your own reason, to come to your own conclusions . . . After all, what laws can be laid down about books?' See Virginia Woolf, *How Should One Read a Book?* (Kindle Edition; first published 1926), loc.1 of 205.

8   See the masterful and beautifully presented work by Keith Houston, entitled *The Book: A Cover-to-Cover Exploration of the Most Powerful Object of Our Time* (New York: W.W. Norton & Company, 2016).

9   Mortimer J. Adler and Charles van Doren wrote a seminal text on this in 1940 entitled *How to Read a Book: The Classic Guide to Intelligent Reading* (New York: Simon & Schuster, 1940).

10 Alberto Manguel is widely regarded as a pioneer in the field on anthology, and has written widely on the history and craft of reading. See, e.g. *A History of Reading* (London: Flamingo, 1992).

11 Damon Young's book *The Art of Reading* (Victoria, Australia: Scribe, 2017), especially Chapter 1, is a helpful modern introduction to such works.

12 See, e.g. https://www.independent.co.uk/voices/comment/poor-reading-skills-are-the-most-serious-weakness-in-our-education-system-8340940.html (accessed 27 April 2020).

13 Flannery O'Connor, 'The Nature and Aims of Fiction' in *Mystery and Manners* (New York: Farrar, Straus and Giroux, 1969), p.80.

14 Victor Hugo, *Les Misérables*, in *The Works of Victor Hugo*, vol. 6, (London: Jenson Society, 1907), p.184.

15 Rabbi Jonathan Sacks, *Lessons in Leadership* (New Milford, CT: Maggid Books & The Orthodox Union, 2015), p.143.

16 American writer Henry Miller possibly has this in mind when he said that 'We should read to give our souls a chance to luxuriate' (source unknown, but widely attributed to Miller). Karen

Swallow Prior writes extensively on this in *On Reading Well: Finding the Good Life through Great Books* (Grand Rapids, MI: Brazos Press, 2018).

[17] In *The Art of Reading, op. cit.*, Damon Young devotes each chapter to a reading virtue.

[18] Christian B. Miller, *The Character Gap: How Good Are We?* (Oxford: Oxford University Press, 2018), especially Chapter 10.

Chapter 1 – The Book

[1] Anne Lamott, *Bird by Bird* (Edinburgh: Canongate, 1994, 2020), p.42. Anne Lamott is an acclaimed American author and fiction-writer.

[2] Orhan Pamuk, *The New Life* (trans. Güneli Gün; London: Faber & Faber, 1997), p.3. Ferit Orhan Pamuk is a Turkish novelist, screenwriter, academic and recipient of the 2006 Nobel Prize in Literature.

[3] Sarah Yardley, MORE > Change (London: Form, 2021), p.56. Sarah is an author, speaker and church leader.

[4] Manguel, *A Reader on Reading*, ix.

[5] For detail on this, see Craig S. Keener, *Acts: An Exegetical Commentary*, vol. 3 (Grand Rapids, MI: Baker Academic, 2014), pp.2855–9.

[6] Widely attributed to Harry Potter series author, J.K. Rowling. See, e.g. https://www.womensweb.in/2018/07/10-jk-rowling-quotes-that-are-not-from-harry-potter-july18wk5sr/ (accessed 2 May 2020). J.K. Rowling is a British author and philanthropist.

[7] Rod Judkins, *The Art of Creative Thinking* (London: Sceptre, 2015), p.202.

[8] See, e.g. https://www.theguardian.com/books/2017/apr/07/the-smell-of-old-books-science-libraries (accessed 15 August 2025).

9   Indexes are more important than some realise. Not only do they help us quickly find things, but a quick scan shows something of the breadth of the book and its content.

10 Philip Pullman, 'Giving books', *The Gifts of Reading* (ed. Robert MacFarlane and Jennie Orchard; London: Weidenfeld & Nicolson, 2020), p.203.

11 William Boyd, 'Some observations on the art and practice of giving books', in *The Gifts of Reading*, ed. MacFarlane and Orchard, p.24.

12 Cited in Jonathan Sacks, *The Power of Ideas* (London: Hodder & Stoughton, 2021), p.113.

13 Sacks, *The Power of Ideas*, p.114.

14 Atheist writer and philosopher Alain de Botton agrees, saying, 'Most of what makes a book good is that we are reading it at the right moment for us', Alan de Botton, Twitter, 20 March 2015. Tim Ferriss makes a similar point in *The Four Hour Workweek*, when he talks of focusing on 'just in time information' rather than accumulating 'just in case information'. See Tim Ferriss, *The Four Hour Workweek* (New York: Crown, 2007), p.92.

15 Manguel, *A Reader on Reading*, p.281.

16 Manguel encourages those looking for what to read to 'trust in pleasure and have faith in haphazardness' (*A Reader on Reading*, p.8).

17 Matthew Porter, *A–Z of Prayer* (Milton Keynes: Authentic Media, 2019), p.209.

18 See, e.g. https://www.understood.org/en/articles/why-reading-in-your-home-language-helps-kids-become-better-readers (accessed 18 August 2025).

19 This is one of the questions I consider in the Appendix, especially at Q.1.

20   Rabbi Jonathan Sacks, *Lessons in Leadership* (New Milford, CT: Maggid Books & The Orthodox Union, 2015).

21   *Surprised by Joy* by C.S. Lewis copyright © 1955 C.S. Lewis Pte. Ltd.

22   Manguel, *A Reader on Reading*, p.238.

Chapter 2 – The Time

1   Confucius (551–479BC) was a Chinese philosopher and politician. Cited in ed. D. Brewer, *Quotes of Confucius And Their Interpretations* (https://www.lulu.com, January 2020), p.113 (accessed 10 March 2023).

2   Ann Voskamp, *One Thousand Gifts* (Grand Rapids, MI: Zondervan, 2010), p.64. Ann Voskamp is a Canadian author, blogger and memoirist on themes of Christian women's spirituality.

3   Erling Kagge, *Silence* (London: Random House, 2017), p.54. Erling Kagge is a Norwegian explorer, publisher, author, lawyer, art collector, entrepreneur and politician.

4   Walter Isaacson, *Steve Jobs* (New York: Little Brown & Company, 2011).

5   I had some family interest in that my father's first computer was an early Apple – back in the late 1980s when few people in the UK owned Apple machines; my wife's uncle had a computing business in Bradford selling Apple products, and my very first computer was an Apple. Also a couple Sam and I knew well were relatives of Jony Ive, Jobs' chief design operator and right-hand man at Apple in California. So I digested the book with vigour, and I certainly wasn't disappointed. Little did I know as I read the book that just over a year later one of the couple related to Jony Ive would die suddenly and I would lead his funeral, and at the wake afterwards I would speak to Jony

about Steve Jobs and the eulogy Jony had given about Steve at Jobs's funeral service the previous year. Reading about Jobs gave me much insight and empathy when I spoke with Jony that following year. In retrospect, it felt like Isaacson's biography had been enlightening and timely, as my reading had prepared me for that conversation.

[6] See https://www.sciencedaily.com/releases/2014/07/140724094209.htm (accessed 10 March 2023). While this book doesn't especially focus on this, many read to learn. Reading helps us understand the world and life better. Leadership expert Nick Lovegrove, for example, enjoys reading obituaries, saying, 'I love to read life stories' not just for inspiration but also to 'learn something every time' (Nick Lovegrove, *The Mosaic Principle* (London: Profile Books, 2017), p.273.

[7] See https://worldliteracyfoundation.org/reading-enhances-imagination/ (accessed 10 March 2023). Alister McGrath summarises this well when he writes that 'Books invite us to imagine new worlds and new ways of thinking', Alister McGrath, *Mere Discipleship: On Growing in Wisdom and Hope* (London: SPCK, 2018), p.58.

[8] See https://www.lucidity.org.uk/5-ways-reading-will-boost-your-communication-skills/ (accessed 10 March 2023).

[9] See https://www.psychologytoday.com/us/blog/socioemotional-success/201707/theory-mind-understanding-others-in-social-world (accessed 10 March 2023).

[10] See https://readingwise.com/blog/what-impact-can-reading-have-on-personality (accessed 10 March 2023).

[11] See https://psycnet.apa.org/record/2000-07037-007 (accessed 10 March 2023).

[12] See https://readingpartners.org/blog/four-compelling-reasons-shut-off-screen-open-good-book (accessed 10 March 2023). Alberto Manguel agrees, noting that 'in moments of darkness we return to books' in *A Reader on Reading*, p.110.

13 See https://www.businessinsider.com/how-to-be-more-interesting-2017-3?r=US&IR=T (accessed 10 March 2023).

14 See https://grottonetwork.com/navigate-life/health-and-wellness/benefits-of-reading/ (accessed 10 March 2023).

15 https://readpraylovedaily.com/page/2/ (accessed 17 April 2020).

16 This is the title of journalist and broadcaster Melvyn Bragg's fascinating book on the Bible. See *The Book of Books* (London: Hodder & Stoughton, 2011).

17 If you want inspiration for using your mornings well, read Allan Jenkins' lovely book, *Morning*. See *Morning: How to Make Time: A Manifesto* (London: Fourth Estate, 2018).

18 See, e.g. https://www.willowshealthcare.com/blog/the-importance-of-a-morning-routine-for-productivity-and-health (accessed 20 August 2025).

19 See his helpful book *Rest* (London: Penguin, 2016), p.25. For further reflection on this, including how great minds have used not just their mornings but all of their day, see Mason Currey, *Daily Rituals: How Great Minds Make Time, Find Inspiration, and Get to Work* (London: Picador, 2013) and Mason Currey, *Daily Rituals: Women at Work* (London: Picador, 2019).

20 See Erling Kagge, *Walking: One Step at a Time* (London: Viking, 2019).

21 See, e.g. Ronald Abadian Heifetz, *The Practice of Adaptive Leadership* (Harvard, MA: Harvard Business Review, 2009), and Nick Lovegrove, *The Mosaic Principle* (London: Profile Books, 2017).

Chapter 3 – The Preparation

1 Ruth Haley Barton, *Strengthening the Soul of Your Leadership* (Downers Grove, IL: IVP Books, 2018), p.70. Barton is an author, teacher, spiritual director and founder of the Transforming Center in Wheaton, Illinois, USA.

2   Cal Newport, *Deep Work: Rules for Focused Success in a Distracted World* (London: Piatkus, 2016), p.134. Calvin C. Newport is an American non-fiction author and associate professor of computer science at Georgetown University, USA.

3   Randy Clark, Afterword in John and Carol Arnott, *Preparing for Glory* (Shippensburg, PA: Destiny Image, 2018), p.191. Randy Clark is a US pastor and author.

4   Mark Batterson, *Win the Day* (Colorado Springs, CO: Multnomah, 2020), p.75.

5   See, e.g. Emily Blatchford, 'Writing By Hand Improves Your Memory, Experts Say' in *Huffington Post*, updated 15.07.16. https://www.huffingtonpost.co.uk/entry/writing-by-hand-improves-your-memory-experts-say_n_61087608e4b0999d2084f66b (accessed 14 April 2020).

6   According to Tim Bouverie, *Allies at War* (London: Bodley Head, 2025). See https://www.theguardian.com/books/2025/apr/08/allies-at-war-politics-of-defeating-hitler-by-tim-bouverie-review-study-of-second-world-war-pacts-is-full-of-surprises (accessed 10 August 2024).

7   *God in the Dock* by C.S. Lewis copyright © 1970 C.S. Lewis Pte. Ltd.

8   Once I realised that a pencil was key to reading, I decided that I wanted to use a *great* pencil, to enhance the reading experience. So a few years ago I spent some time researching and I ended up choosing the Kerry mechanical pencil. Not only is it stylish and beautiful, but it is highly functional, doesn't need sharpening and the leads rarely break. It also has a lid, like an ink pen, so you can carry it in your pocket without spiking yourself on the sharp end. Although it takes a little time to order, as it usually needs importing from Japan, it's not expensive – it's just a great pencil. I like it so much I've bought most of my family one too. Of course, you don't need to use a Kerry.

9   For more on distractions and living intentionally, see, e.g. Newport, *Deep Work*.

10 Henry David Thoreau, *Walden* (Yale, MA: Yale University Press, 2004), p.xx.

11 Jonathan Haidt, *The Anxious Generation* (London: Allen Lane, 2024).

12 While I advise people to approach reading with an open attitude, it's also good to recognise the beliefs, experiences and worldviews that we bring to reading. Reading books that challenge these things can be healthy and it's good to take note of any negative reactions to things we read. However, sometimes it's OK to stop reading something because you find it offensive, distasteful or just unhelpful. Occasionally I start reading and decide not to continue. That's not, I trust, because I'm narrow-minded or being judgemental of the author but because I want the learning experience to be formative. In the end, I must take care about what I read, because the quality of my reading shapes the quality of my thinking and my living.

13 Many studies lean to this understanding. These include: https://scholarsarchive.byu.edu/cgi/viewcontent.cgi?article=6805&-context=facpub (accessed 21 August 2025).

14 See, e.g. Eph. 4:4; 2 Cor. 3:12; Heb. 6:19 and Jer. 29:11.

15 Anne Lamott, *Bird by Bird* (Edinburgh: Canongate, 1994, 2020), p.17.

16 Many novelists admit to this. See, e.g. Simon Akam and Rachel Lloyd, *Always Take Notes* (London: Ithaka, 2024).

17 In coming years, as Artificial Intelligence improves, many will increasingly ask, 'Did a human write this?'

18 Stating on the back cover of their books: 'Our passion is to produce resources that build up the body of Christ, promoting spiritual growth, wisdom, mission and creativity.'

[19]　McGrath, *Mere Discipleship*, p.142.

[20]　Cited in Melvyn Bragg, *The Book of Books* (London: Hodder, 2011), p.7.

[21]　https://www.churchofengland.org/prayer-and-worship/worship-texts-and-resources/common-worship/ministry/common-worship-ordination-0 (accessed 12 August 2025).

[22]　https://www.churchofengland.org/prayer-and-worship/worship-texts-and-resources/common-worship/ministry/common-worship-ordination-0. See Notes, section 13 (accessed 21 November 2025).

[23]　See, e.g. 2 Tim. 3:16–17; John 20:30–31.

[24]　Matthew Porter, *A–Z of Discipleship* (Milton Keynes: Authentic Media, 2017), p.81. In essence, we need to learn to read the Bible well, so we can apply it practically to our lives, so we can do the basic things of the faith, like: love God and love people (Matt. 22:37); share the good news of Jesus (Matt. 28:18–20) and live generously and care for people in poverty (1 John 3:17).

Chapter 4 – The Aim

[1]　Edward O. Wilson, *Consilience: The Unity of Knowledge* (New York: Vintage, 1999), p.294. Edward Wilson was an academic and deep thinker; he was a Pulitzer Prize-winning author and known for particularly developing the field of sociobiology.

[2]　Hannah Steele, *Living His Story* (London: SPCK, 2020), p.86. Hannah Steele is a church leader, theologian and author.

[3]　Widely attributed to Irish politician and playwright Richard Steele (1672–1729). See, e.g. http://www.bristol.ac.uk/media-library/sites/sps/migrated/documents/section4.pdf (accessed 2 May 2020).

4   See, e.g. https://medium.com/@kevinnokiawriting/why-build-ing-a-reading-habit-can-transform-your-life-c2214377dfa8 (accessed 16 August 2025). American writer and editor Damon Young agrees, saying: 'To read well, I have to *read*: widely and carefully, mindful of my powers and responsibilities' (*The Art of Reading*, p.16).

5   Boyd, 'Some observations on the art and practice of giving books', in *The Gifts of Reading*, ed. MacFarlane and Orchard, ed. Robert MacFarlane and Jennie Orchard, *The Gifts of Reading* (London: Weidenfeld & Nicolson, 2020), p.25.

6   See https://www.bbc.co.uk/culture/article/20180503-our-fiction-addiction-why-humans-need-stories (accessed 7 August 2025).

7   See, e.g. https://medium.com/the-mission/the-importance-of-reading-fiction-7f57546a229b (accessed 7 August 2025), and https://greatergood.berkeley.edu/article/item/how_reading_fiction_can_shape_our_real_lives (accessed 7 August 2025).

8   I work closely with Rachel Mann in my role as Bishop of Bolton. Rachel is an acclaimed author and poet, one of only ten authors to be nominated for the 2025 T.S. Eliot Prize for Poetry.

9   I like Michael Yankoski's insights into attentiveness. Rather than encouraging people to 'pay attention' he prefers the call to 'be attentive' saying that 'attentiveness is not something you can buy at any price but rather something you must become. Attentive is a way of being in the world, an inherent availability and receptivity, a connection . . .' See Michael Yankoski, *The Sacred Year* (Nashville, TN: Thomas Nelson, 2014), p.25.

10   David Watson wrote a number of books, including classics such as *You Are My God* (London: Hodder & Stoughton, 1983) and *Fear No Evil* (London: Hodder & Stoughton, 1984).

11   Paula Gooder, *Journalling the Psalms* (London: Hodder & Stoughton, 2022), p.6.

[12] Eugene Peterson helpfully notes: 'The comprehensiveness of these five witnesses becomes evident when we set Psalms as the centre and then crisscross that centre with the other four books arranged as two sets of polarities: Song of Solomon and Job, then Proverbs and Ecclesiastes. Psalms is the magnetic centre, pulling every scrap and dimension of human experience into a prayerful response to God.' For more on this, see Eugene Peterson, *As Kingfishers Catch Fire* (Colorado Springs, CO: WaterBrook, 2017), p.166ff.

[13] See, e.g. John H. Darch and Stuart K. Burns, *Saints on Earth: A Biographical Companion to Common Worship* (London: Church House Publishing, 2017), p.28.

[14] Ps. 103:7. We particularly discover the centrality of Christ, and how through his life, death, resurrection and ascension, Jesus has changed the world and offers all people new identity and a new hope.

[15] See 1 Kgs 3.

[16] See Matt. 7:24–27. See also Matt. 11:19, where Jesus says that 'wisdom is proved right by her deeds'.

[17] Cited by Hannah Heather, in her Study Guide in Pete Greig, *Dirty Glory* (London: Hodder & Stoughton, 2016), p.339.

[18] Author and pastor Eugene Peterson agrees, saying: 'Reading is an immense gift, but only if the words are assimilated, taken into the soul – eaten, chewed, gnawed, received in unhurried delight.' Eugene Peterson, *Eat This Book* (London: Hodder & Stoughton, 2006), p.11.

[19] See https://www.ignatianspirituality.com/ignatian-prayer/the-what-how-why-of-prayer/praying-with-scripture/ (accessed 10 March 2023).

[20] Luke 5:17–26.

21   See https://radical.net/article/dont-simply-read-through-the-bible-meditate-on-it/ (accessed 10 March 2023).

22   J.R.R. Tolkien, *The Fellowship of the Ring* (New York: Harper Collins, 1991), p.48.

23   See 2 Peter 3:1, where Peter says: 'Dear friends, this is now my second letter to you. I have written both of them as reminders to stimulate you to wholesome thinking.'

24   Austin Farrer, *The Glass of Vision* (Westminster: Dacre, 1948), p.36.

25   Reflecting on the Torah, the first five books of the Bible, Rabbi Jonathan Sacks says that 'Torah is written to be read aloud', Rabbi Jonathan Sacks, *Genesis: The Book of Beginnings* (New Milford, CT: Maggid Books & The Orthodox Union, 2009), p. 204. For more on reading literature out loud, see https://www.the-guardian.com/books/2019/mar/09/why-reading-aloud-is-a-vi-tal-bridge-to-literacy (accessed 29 September 2024).

26   S.F. Said, 'The best gifts you can give' in *The Gifts of Reading*, ed. MacFarlane and Orchard, pp. 242–3.

27   See, e.g. Augustine Sedgewick, *Fatherhood: A History of Love and Power* (London: Picador, 2025), p.157.

28   For more on this, and particularly on the difference between writing and speaking, see, e.g.: https://www.futurity.org/brains-speech-writ-ing-communication-919852/ (accessed 14 April 2020).

29   See my reading of *A–Z of Discipleship*, at https://www.youtube.com/watch?v=HLkUJGqOjYs (accessed 12 August 2025).

30   See, e.g. Gus Palmer, 'Power of the Spoken Word'. *American Indian Quarterly,* vol. 38, no. 4 (Fall 2014): pp. 512–23, https://doi.org/10.5250/amerindiquar.38.4.0512 (accessed 11 May 2024), and Lori M. Walkington, 'The Power of Spoken-Word: Transformative Social Justice and Healing in Structurally Oppressed Communities', https://escholarship.org/uc/item/41f546x9 (accessed 11 May 2024).

Chapter 5 – The End

1. Widely attributed to Irish statesman and philosopher Edmund Burke (1729–97). See, e.g. Katherine Wiesolek Kuta, *Reading and Writing to Learn* (London: Teacher Ideas Press, 2008) p.49.

2. Stephen Cottrell, *Hit the Ground Kneeling* (London: Church House Publishing, 2008), p.16. Stephen Cottrell is the Archbishop of York at the time of writing.

3. Thomas Merton, *New Seeds of Contemplation* (New York: New Directions Publishing Corporation, 1961), p.98. Merton (1915–68) was an American Trappist monk, author and poet.

4. See, e.g. Brené Brown, *Daring Greatly* (New York: Penguin, 2012).

5. See Alex Ferguson with Michael Moritz, *Leading* (London: Hodder & Stoughton, 2015).

6. See https://evernote.com (accessed 7 November 2025).

7. See Matthew Porter, *The Art of Journalling: Becoming a More Reflective Person* (Milton Keynes: Authentic, 2024).

8. Sisonke Msimang, 'The solace of Sundays', in *The Gifts of Reading*, ed. MacFarlane and Orchard, p.143.

9. Keith Ng, 'Keep Calm and Kondo On', article in *The Telegraph Magazine*, 11 April 2020, p.11.

10. Robert Poynton, *Do/Pause* (London: Do Book Co., 2019), p.58. Poynton is a facilitator, coach, author and creative business thinker.

Chapter 6 – The Return

1. *God in the Dock* by C.S. Lewis copyright © 1970 C.S. Lewis Pte. Ltd. Clive Staples Lewis (1898–1963) was a British writer and Anglican lay theologian, who held academic positions in English literature at both the University of Oxford and the University of Cambridge.

2 Lloyd Alexander (1924–2007) was an American author who wrote for more than seven decades. See transcript of interview in: https://www.scholastic.com/teachers/articles/teaching-content/lloyd-alexander-interview-transcript/ (accessed 2 May 2020).

3 Author unknown. In *More Than Words* – article in *The Sunday Times Magazine*, 19 April 2009, p.8, Queen Rania of Jordan describes the words coming from a South African author.

4 Manguel, *A Reader on Reading*, p.4.

5 Manguel, *ibid.*, x.

6 See Young, *The Art of Reading*, p.34.

7 *They Stand Together* by C.S. Lewis copyright © 1979 C.S. Lewis Pte. Ltd.

8 Manguel, *A Reader on Reading*, p.289. Most writers are avid readers, with children's author S.F. Said noting: 'All writers are really readers who take one more step, and pass on what they've received, adding something of their own along the way.' S.F. Said, 'The best gifts you can give,' in *The Gifts of Reading*, ed. MacFarlane and Orchard, p.245.

9 Henry Kissinger, *Leadership* (London: Allen Lane, 2022), pp. 405–6.

10 John Wesley, cited in *English Spirituality in the Age of Wesley* (ed. David Lyle Jeffrey; Grand Rapids, MI: Eerdmans, 1987), p.30.

11 Young, *The Art of Reading*, p.6.

12 McGrath, *Mere Discipleship*, p.73.

13 John Wesley, cited in *English Spirituality in the Age of Wesley*, ed. Jeffrey, p.30. John Wesley (1703–91) was an English cleric, theologian and evangelist who was a leader of a revival movement within the Church of England known as Methodism. The societies he founded became the dominant form of the independent Methodist movement that continues to this day.

Afterword

[1] Source unknown but widely attributed to Mary McLeod Bethune (1875–1955), an important black educator, civil and women's rights leader and government official in the United States. The college she founded set educational standards for colleges, and her role as an advisor to President Franklin Roosevelt gave African Americans an advocate in government. Cited, for example, by President Bill Clinton, see https://clinton. presidentiallibraries.us/items/show/47613 (accessed 13 October 2025). Office of Speechwriting and Lowell Weiss, 'Lighthouse School', *Clinton Digital Library*.

[2] Widely attributed to Emerson. Source unknown. Ralph Waldo Emerson (1803–82) was a nineteenth-century American essayist, philosopher and poet.

[3] Widely attributed to Kennedy. Source unknown. Jackie Kennedy Onassis (1929–94) was an American socialite, writer, photographer and book editor who served as the first lady of the United States from 1961 to 1963, as the wife of President John F. Kennedy.

[4] Marilynne Robinson, *When I Was a Child I Read Books* (New York: Farrar, Straus & Giroux, 2012), p.85.

[5] Because Revelation 20:12 describes not only 'the book of life' being opened and read but also other books. It may well be that we have lots of time for reading in eternity.

Appendix

[1] Jancis Robinson notes this, saying, 'So how do we decide which books to read? Recommendations from friends are surely the surest source', Jancis Robinson, 'Vintage reading' in *The Gifts of Reading*, ed. MacFarlane and Orchard, p.229.

[2] *Mere Christianity* by C.S. Lewis copyright © 1942, 1943, 1944, 1952 C.S. Lewis Pte. Ltd.

[3] See Matt. 6:22; Luke 6:45.

Index

The Art of Giving

Becoming a more generous person

Matthew Porter

Why is it good to give?

How does it change me and impact the world?

Why is giving so central to the life of the follower of Jesus?

Whether you want help on how to start giving or how to be a more generous giver, *The Art of Giving* is a practical and accessible guide that will help you draw closer to God through the practice of joyful generosity.

978-1-78893-290-5

The Art of Journalling

Becoming a more reflective person

Matthew Porter

What is the value of journalling?

How does it change me and help me make a difference in the world?

Do you want to start journalling but don't know how?

Whether you want help on how to start journalling, or looking for how to do it better, *The Art of Journalling* is a practical and accessible guide that will help you draw closer to God through the practice of reflective writing.

978-1-78893-288-2

The Art of Fasting

Becoming a more prayerful person

Matthew Porter

What is the point of fasting?

How does it change me and help me make a difference in the world?

Do you want to start fasting but don't know how?

Whether you want help on how to start fasting or how to develop a more prayerful approach, *The Art of Fasting* is a practical and accessible guide that will help you draw closer to God through the practice of intentional fasting.

978-1-78893-369-8

A-Z of Discipleship

Building strong foundations for a life of following Jesus

Matthew Porter

How do I live out my Christian faith?

A-Z of Discipleship is an accessible introduction to the understanding and practice of the Christian faith. It presents twenty-six aspects of discipleship to help you grow in your relationship with God, connect with church and live as a follower of Christ in contemporary culture.

978-1-78078-456-4

A-Z of Prayer

Building strong foundations for daily conversations with God

Matthew Porter

How do I pray?

A-Z of Prayer is an accessible introduction that gives practical guidance on how to develop a meaningful prayer life. It presents twenty-six aspects of prayer to help you grow in your relationship with God, explore new devotional styles and deepen your daily conversations with God.

978-1-78893-062-8

A-Z of Wellbeing

*Finding your personal toolkit for
peace and wholeness*

Ruth Rice

How do I look after my mental health?

A-Z of Wellbeing is an accessible introduction to help you attend to
your own wellbeing and live out your own alphabet of peace. It presents twenty-six words of wellness to help you discover new practices,
connect with God, and find your own toolkit of words and habits that
will help you maintain your own wellbeing.

978-1-78893-237-0

Authentic

We trust you enjoyed reading this book
from Authentic. If you want to be
informed of any new titles from this author
and other releases you can sign up to the
Authentic newsletter by scanning below:

Online:
authenticmedia.co.uk

Follow us: